Tired of Apologizing
for a Church
I Don't Belong To

Also by Lillian Daniel

When "Spiritual but Not Religious" Is Not Enough: Seeing God in Surprising Places, Even the Church

Tell It Like It Is: Reclaiming the Practice of Testimony

This Odd and Wondrous Calling: The Public and Private Lives of Two Ministers

Tired of Apologizing for a Church I Don't Belong To

Spirituality without Stereotypes, Religion without Ranting

LILLIAN DANIEL

New York   Boston   Nashville

FaithWords
Hachette Book Group
1290 Avenue of the Americas, New York, NY 10104
faithwords.com
twitter.com/faithwords

First Edition: September 2016

FaithWords is a division of Hachette Book Group, Inc. The FaithWords
name and logo are trademarks of Hachette Book Group, Inc.

The publisher is not responsible for websites (or their content) that are
not owned by the publisher.

The Hachette Speakers Bureau provides a wide range of authors for
speaking events. To find out more, go to www.hachettespeakersbureau
.com or call (866) 376-6591.

Library of Congress Cataloging-in-Publication Data has been applied for.

ISBNs: 978-1-4555-9589-1 (hardcover), 978-1-4555-9590-7 (ebook), 978-1-
4789-1270-5 (audiobook, downloadable)

Printed in the United States of America

RRD-C

10   9   8   7   6   5   4   3   2   1

Contents

Contents

The Guest House

This being human is a guest house.
Every morning a new arrival.
A joy, a depression, a meanness,
some momentary awareness comes
as an unexpected visitor.
Welcome and entertain them all!

RUMI, 1207–1273

Part I

SPIRITUALITY WITHOUT STEREOTYPES

Arguments for atheism can be divided into two main categories: those that dispute the existence of god and those that demonstrate the ill effects of religion. CHRISTOPHER HITCHENS, 1949–2011

We have to stop saying when something like this that happened in Paris today, we have to stop saying, well, we should not insult a great religion. First of all, there are no great religions. They're all stupid and dangerous—and we should insult them and we should be able to insult whatever we want. That is what free speech is like. BILL MAHER, 1956–

I kind of thought it was the job of a chaplain to be insensitive to atheists.   TED CRUZ, 1970–

Look at these Christians, how they love one another.
                                     TERTULLIAN, 160–220

Why can't the freedom to acknowledge God be enjoyed again by children in every schoolroom across this land?
                    PRESIDENT RONALD REAGAN, 1911–2004

Hi I'm Ron Reagan....lifelong atheist, not afraid of burning in hell.   RON REAGAN JR., 1958–

I do not fear Satan half so much as I fear those who fear him.   TERESA OF AVILA, 1514–1582

Believe me, if I run and I win, I will be the greatest representative of the Christians they've had in a long time.   DONALD TRUMP, 1946–

In heaven, all the interesting people are missing.
                       FRIEDRICH NIETZSCHE, 1844–1900

Chapter 1

My Multifaith Moment at Marshall's

WHEN A STRANGER STARTED TALKING to me in the long checkout line at Marshall's, I welcomed the distraction. We commiserated about the inefficiencies of the system and both swore we wouldn't be coming back to this store again. In other words, we exchanged pleasantries and lied to each other.

But as the time passed, both of us standing there with nothing to do, he started to talk about real things. It was one of those strangely intimate meetings. He wanted to talk, I was ready to listen, and the lady in front of us was processing a massive return from an earlier bad shopping day.

Before we started talking, I had noticed that he was wearing a turban, a sign of Sikh religion. But we weren't talking about religion, thank God. Standing in line in the suburbs of Chicago, he told me he had been raised in India, moved to Chicago as an adult, but now most of his family lived in London. That included his favorite elderly aunt, a woman who was dearer to him than any living relative. Now she was dying, across the ocean in London, and he was trying to figure out whether to purchase an incredibly expensive airline ticket right away so that he could go to his aunt's dying bedside before she passed away, or whether he should wait and fly to London later, for her inevitable funeral.

"What would you do?" he asked me with a catch in his throat.

His emotion and openness startled me, so I deflected by asking more questions, heading straight to the land of logistics, where I was more comfortable. Could he make two trips? What were the family's expectations? Was his aunt alone or did she have others by her side? Had he heard about the various discount air travel websites? Why not make both trips? What exactly was his financial situation?

"Well, I'm shopping at Marshall's!" he replied, and that made us both laugh. He knew he could not afford to go to London twice. He could barely afford to go once. Last-minute airline travel is expensive. Like most people, he was on a budget, hence his presence at an understaffed discount store. He had to make a choice.

Should he break the bank to buy the last-minute ticket that would get him to her dying bedside in twenty-four hours and say good-bye to his aunt in person? Or should he save the money and plan ahead, to go to London for the funeral, when the rest of the family would be there? He was really wrestling with this, trying to make a decision.

Once I realized I couldn't solve his problem with obvious answers and travel tips, we talked more deeply. Knowing he could make only one trip, he was leaning toward making the trip the next day, to be in her presence, despite the enormous expense. I told him about all the times I had visited my mother when she was dying, when it felt like I was using the airplane like a bus, racking up credit card bills, never knowing if this visit would be the last. At least she and I had been in the same country. His situation was harder. But I told him I was glad I had gone.

Then, in the interest of honesty, I felt I should tell him about the other times when I had chosen not to do something. Looking back, there were plenty of things I had missed—weddings, funerals, celebrations, crises—all for good reasons like money, work, and family. Even though I had my sensible reasons for missing those things, when I look back today, I can't remember what exactly they were. Whatever the reasons, they weren't important enough to withstand the test of time.

What I do recall are the feelings of regret that remain with me to this day. Work deadlines and family sports schedules that seemed so urgent at the time fade, but those "big things" are the bright lights that stay turned on in our memories and remind us we were alive. I should have gone to most of them. He nodded as if he had been right there with me, and said, "I want to see my aunt while she is still alive. I want to remember."

Suddenly a flashing light above the cashier's head broke our connection. "I can help you down here at number five, sir," she called, and with that, we were separated, he to his payment station and me to mine. It seemed too abrupt but we moved as instructed. My cart was full of items that looked unfamiliar to me. Why did I think I needed these things? They were useless, cold, and plastic. I was having trouble remembering why I thought I needed them in the first place. As I picked up my receipt, I knew it was time to leave, but I didn't want to go without saying something to this man whose story hung between us. As he collected his receipt, I tapped his shoulder and said, "Hey, I'm going to pray for you, and for your aunt."

I wish I could tell you that his eyes lit up with joy at our powerful connection but it was quite different. He pulled back almost in horror, and backed away from me. I felt terrible, as if I had poisoned this beautiful moment. But what poisoned it? I knew it was my announcement that I would pray for him. I was mad at myself. I had to introduce that religion thing, right?

Besides, I could have just prayed for him without an accompanying announcement. Prayers still work when you don't brag about performing them. In fact, if you take

Jesus' word for it, they work better that way. I didn't have to blow the whole moment. I made this poor man uncomfortable. My words were like a roll call at the dentist's office; no one wants to be in line for what's next. My prayer plans made him back away from me.

He was out in the parking lot before I was, no doubt rushing to his phone to tell someone in India that yet another obnoxious American had tried to convert him.

He probably associated the phrase "I'll pray for you" with other Christians who had said that to him and judged him for his Sikh religion.

Was I saying, "I'll pray for you," because I wanted to convert him? Was I saying, "I'll pray for you," because I was judging him in some way? Was I praying for him in a condescending way, as if my prayers would work better than his, so he could relax now that a professional was on it? He had every right to say, "Wait a second, lady, don't you assume that we believe the same thing." And that could well have been true, but I didn't care. I wanted to pray for him to let him know that I valued him and the tender story he had told me. It had nothing to do with belief in my faith or his. But clearly that hadn't come through. I pushed my cart full of crap to my car, and clicked open the trunk, only to discover it was already full of other things I didn't need.

Just then I heard these running steps behind me, and a screech of a grocery cart pulled to a stop, and it was him. He'd run outside after me. "I wanted to say thank you," he said.

"I wanted to apologize," I said.

"For what?" he asked.

"For saying I'd pray for you, for the Christian Church, for whoever said that to you in your past and didn't mean it, or for whoever said it and did mean it but wanted to convert you. I want to apologize for all the religious whack jobs out there in the world and for the disproportionate number of them who attend church in the western suburbs of Chicago. I want to apologize for how the Sikh people have been treated. I want to apologize for the high price of air travel, for the fact that your aunt is so terribly sick, and for the long line at Marshall's, too."

"That's a lot to apologize for," he said, looking rather stunned. "So you're responsible for all of that?" And then we laughed.

Chapter 2

Tired of Apologizing

I USED TO DO THAT, apologizing for this, that, and the other thing, in order to demonstrate I was "not that kind of Christian." Religion bashers had nothing on me. I would beat them to the punch, giving them things the church should apologize for that they hadn't even thought of yet.

"The Inquisition? Don't even bring it up; I'm way ahead of you. I was mad about it before you even heard of it, that's how open-minded I am. Salem witch trials? I know! So embarrassing. Can I hang out with you anyway? You're too kind."

"Religion is responsible for all the wars in history," they would say, and I'd respond, "You're so right. Don't forget imperialism, capitalism, and racism. Religion invented those problems, too. You can tell that because religious people can be found at all their meetings."

And by the way, I am a pastor. Pastors love Jesus so much we're willing to accept a salary for it. I have been one for a couple of decades. And before that, I was a Christian, the regular kind who doesn't get paid for it. But don't hold it against me. I can apologize for being a pastor, too, if you like. Lord knows I've done it before.

Why *is* that?

Why do I—why do so many believers—feel that we're inherently responsible for every single unchristian thing ever done by anyone who ever called themselves Christian? After all, Christianity is a pretty big category; in the United States alone there are more than 1,500 Christian denominations. Imagine that—one thousand five hundred groups decided they couldn't abide their community of faith, so they started their own. Obviously these denominations don't all believe the same things or behave the same way. So why should any Christian feel the need to apologize on behalf of strangers? Or even distant relatives?

If Christianity were a country—let's call it France just for now—what would you think if someone told you this about his or her experience there? "I've been to France, and I didn't enjoy it. In fact, I got nothing out of it. I would never go back to France. The French people, I mean...they claim to care about fashion, but I saw some of them wearing unflattering hemlines. They claim to want everyone to see Paris, but then I got there and the Parisians all ignored me. When I asked for directions, they were snooty and talked back to me in French, which is impossible to understand. Later I read about the French and how they started all these wars and had a history of not giving people directions. Don't even get me started. I hate France and all it stands for. In fact, I'm just offended anyone would even suggest I go to France. To be honest, I'm shocked that you go to France. You seem so...not French. How can you live with yourself?"

What if they went on to say, "I will now never visit any country in the continent of Europe because I object to the behavior of its leaders, and Europeans started wars, too, no doubt influenced by the French. And I'm not making this up, I've been to France, and as I explained, I hated it on a personal as well as an intellectual level. And quite frankly, I can't believe a thoughtful person like you wouldn't object to the whole continent either..."

Why, if someone said that to you, you'd call them out on their bigotry. You would explain that the continent and its people are diverse and complex. And if you had ever lived in one of those countries and loved it, you might encourage them to try it out, too.

If somebody talked like that, you'd say, "That's insane. You can't talk like that about the people of France. You went one time. Give it a chance."

"Nope."

"But there are wonderful things in France."

"Don't push France down my throat."

Gulp. "Okay, I'm sorry."

"Stop trying to brainwash me!"

Double gulp. "Really sorry."

"Well it's too late to apologize because this is exactly what you French people do and this is why we hate you!"

Fair enough. But is it?

What do you say to that? It's a crazy way of talking that we would not tolerate in any other context. That's the talk I want to push back against these days. But where do I begin? It's complicated.

First, I can't speak up for all of Christianity. I can't speak for all of high school. I can't speak for everybody in France. There are some people in France I'm not crazy about either. I've had my own experiences in high school. Those arguments are exhausting and rarely fruitful.

But second, I want to speak up in some way. I am tired of saying nothing, or apologizing. And I don't think I'm alone.

For a long time, open-minded religious people have said nothing, or very little. We tune out the ranting about religion. We hope that by saying nothing, people will see that we are not so bad after all.

But when you just heard that talk being applied to France, didn't it get your hackles up just a bit? Didn't you want to defend those folks?

I find that I'm more comfortable getting mad about the people of France because I am not one of them. I don't have a vested interest in you liking France. I just know you shouldn't stereotype a whole group of people like that.

My friend from New York City vividly describes the aftermath of 9/11 in her borough of Queens, which is, according to *The Guinness Book of World Records*, the most ethnically diverse place on the planet. More than 160 languages are spoken in the 109 square miles that comprise Queens. Usually a bragging point among the residents, that same diversity became a painful experience for her and for many of her neighbors.

She felt like Osama bin Laden's Al-Qaeda singlehandedly made all Muslims "the potential enemy" in America, and especially in New York. Suddenly every person in Islamic garb was a "suspect," even in Queens.

That had abated to some degree in New York City in the ensuing fifteen years. But then the 2016 presidential race triggered a new spate of hateful anti-Muslim behavior in an election season when Donald Trump advocated the banning of all Muslims from America "until we can sort things out."

My New York friend, a practicing Christian and a liberal Democrat, started feeling the need to apologize to the Muslims she encountered—friends, neighbors, and even strangers—for the behavior of Christians who were supporting candidates like Trump.

It occurred to me that she isn't the only one compelled to apologize.

How many times have you seen a Muslim man or woman on TV standing behind a podium at a news conference following some atrocity like the massacre in San Bernardino? "We're not like them," the Muslims would say of the shooters. "Islam is a peaceful religion. Our imams condemn violence.

Really—those people are members of a group that thinks it's Muslim, or claims it. But they're not one of us."

When I see Muslims having to defend themselves like that, it infuriates me as it infuriates my friend from Queens. They shouldn't have to state their case over and against the crazies. They shouldn't have to deal with those stereotypes.

So why do I tolerate the stereotyping of my own people, and my own community of faith? And when did I start apologizing for a church I don't belong to? I think it grew from a spirit of wanting to make room for many paths, and wanting to live that out. It grew from good values that came to me from being a part of a religious community that followed Jesus who welcomed the outsiders.

But somewhere along the path of life in religious community, I got confused about what to say to other people, and I don't think I'm alone. I stopped speaking honestly about what was dear to me, started apologizing and sometimes just got stuck in silence. When I look back on it today, I recall my journey like a parable, an exaggerated, comical story that makes a point or two along the way.

Many paths—a parable

I believe that there are many paths to God. I just don't trust all the signage. But I do trust that there is more than one way to get from point A to point B. You're more likely to get there if you don't constantly jump from path to path. There's value in going deeply into one path and still being glad for the other routes out there. But as we walk our paths, and notice that there is more than one path, do we simply pass one another at the intersection and wave? Sometimes people do need to switch paths, or get on one for the first time. So what if we catch someone looking curiously at our path, with questions. They might even look longingly at it. They might put out a foot and try to step onto it.

In the past, as an open-minded Christian, I felt it was my job to stop them from doing that. First, I needed to tell them what they were getting into. Then I had to apologize in advance for all the other people on the path that they would run into. And of course, I had to apologize for the path's graduates and alumni, who give enlightened people like me a bad name.

Don't get on this path too quick now. We've burned witches here. I'm sorry but it's true. Furthermore, we've tortured people, from the Tower of London to megachurch infomercials, we are guilty.

Apologizing for every bad thing done in the name of religion is an exhausting task. I wasn't always up for it. Sometimes it was easier to pretend I wasn't on the path, so I wouldn't have to cover all that material.

Sometimes I'd walk straight by that curious person. I'd keep my head down and my eyes on the road right under my plodding feet, and hope that by ignoring them, I'd convey how accepting I was of their nonparticipation on my path, which really was no better than any other path. Worse, maybe.

But even then, they might want more. They might run alongside me, catch up to me, and ask me why I am so intent on this particular path. I may be tired of apologizing but at least I'm not participating in false advertising. "Well, this path is no better than any other one," I reply. And I feel good about it. I imagine the curious guy feels good about it, too. I have neglected to apologize but have demonstrated how open-minded I am.

I have conveyed that I'm not like those other types of Christians on the path that is way over there to the right, the judgmental ones. I don't insist that you get on my path for your own salvation. I don't even claim my path is a better one.

But I've gotten tired of apologizing for a church I'm not a member of. I'm tired of giving the conversation about faith over to the extremists, and letting them define me. I believe you can be an open-minded Christian, who thinks God can work out everyone's salvation. We human beings don't need to get all worked up on God's behalf. God has this covered. Walk your path and enjoy the view.

That's my path and I didn't invent it. It's been around for a while. There have always been strains of Christianity that denigrate other paths. And there have always been strains that delight in every alternate route, exit, and off-ramp.

You can find the same variety of paths in other religions. Paths are as diverse as the people who follow them.

It's easy to point to the problems on someone else's

path. You'll always find wrecks on the side of the road. That's what happens when you open the path up to the public, otherwise known as other people.

Yes, we mess things up a lot on the Christian path. We litter, we speed, we crash our cars, and sometimes we even run over armadillos and bunnies. If you let my father on your path, he will go everywhere and do everything at 30 miles an hour: forward, reverse, left turn, right turn, all at 30 miles per hour. The path would be safer without him on it, but it's a public thoroughfare.

So don't point out roadkill and then tell me that "the road" has it in for bunnies, deer, and armadillos. Don't ask me to defend transportation because there are bad drivers on the road. Don't tell me that roads are responsible for all the wars in history. Without roads, we'd still have wars. We'd just stay at home and fight with our neighbors.

Chapter 3

Tongue-Tied in a "Spiritual but Not Religious" World

A FEW YEARS AGO, I drew some flack for a short *Huffington Post* piece, entitled "Spiritual but Not Religious? Please Stop Boring Me." I explained that I was tired of spiritual but not religious people who think they are unique, daring, or interesting because they find God in the sunset. "Thank you for sharing, spiritual but not religious sunset person." I wrote, "You are now comfortably in the norm for self-centered American culture, right smack in the bland majority of people who find ancient religions dull but find themselves uniquely fascinating."

My take is that anyone can find God in the sunset. What is *remarkable* is finding God in the context of flawed human community, in a tradition bigger than you are, with people who may not reflect God back to you in your own image.

I followed that article with a much longer piece in the *Christian Century Magazine* that argued the point more thoroughly. It was called "You Can't Make This Stuff Up: The Limits of Self-Made Religion." And in it I suggested, "At some point, if you think about it at all, that person with the self-made religion will use his God-given brain and the wisdom of hard experiences, and start to ask angry and provocative questions of this spirituality of status quo, like: 'Who are you, God of sunsets, and rainbows, and bunnies and chain e-mails about sweet friends? Who are you, cheap God of self-satisfaction and isolation? Who are you, God of the beautiful and the physically fit? Who are you, God of the spiritual and not religious? Who are you, God of the lucky, chief priest of the religion of gratitude? Who are you and are you even worth knowing? Who are you, God who I invent? Is there, could there be, a more interesting God who invented me?' "

Both articles went viral, initially sent out by folks who liked them, then responded to by people who did not. I got more hate mail over those pieces than anything I've ever written. Who knew so many atheists read religion blog posts? And at risk of ticking them off all over again, I decided to turn all that into a book called *When "Spiritual but Not Religious" Is Not Enough: Seeing God in Surprising Places, Even the Church.*

When you put *"Spiritual but Not Religious"* in your book

title, you can't be shocked when you start hearing from them. And I did. For the most part these self-described SBNRs wanted to make a case for why what they were doing was based in God, community, and a tradition larger than themselves. Most of what they were doing sounded good to me. So what if they didn't call it "religion," even though I was often pointing out that the root of the word "religion" is just community, which they seemed to be in favor of?

I continued to disagree with the solitary SBNRs who took potshots at organized religion and I heard from them. I questioned their terminal uniqueness and pointed out that they were now in the growing majority of American culture. This elicited a howl of complaints. Say what you want about the growing numbers of SBNRs, they don't want to hear that they are growing in number and are commonplace in their views. They want to be on the fringe and cutting edge.

Daffodils

When I was a child, my mother planned a big garden party. At the heart of her vision was that our backyard would be filled with blooming daffodils, which she had planted in anticipation of this party long before. But as the party date approached, the weather stayed cold and no daffodils were even close to blooming.

Yet on the day of the party, our lawn was filled with daffodils, just as she had dreamed. The guests marveled at the springtime beauty of our yard, especially since no garden in the neighborhood had any springtime action like that.

But then after the guests went home, the daffodils drooped and my mother went through the yard carefully removing all the cut daffodils she had bought at the florist, that she had painstakingly attached to chopsticks with wire twist ties, that she had then carefully stuck in the ground.

Those daffodils weren't fake; they were just short-lived and flimsy, with no bulb under the earth to allow them to survive the rough weather. On the surface and for a short while, they looked like real daffodils but they didn't have enough going on underneath to last. My mother's daffodils were like many SBNRs' beliefs, chosen because they are pretty blossoms that were real, but they weren't living. They weren't rooted; they wilted early on because there was no oxygen to sustain them. As an SBNR, you can go to the religious flower shop, and pick up a little of this and a little of that, and decorate your life with it. You can visit this religious community with its art and watch a documentary about another one with a lovely view. You can read this deep thinker and the next. You can say you believe in a thousand wise sayings and make yourself your own pretty bouquet of blossoms, all ready for the party or the picnic on a sunny day. But life is not a picnic. And the people who finally dig in and put down roots in one tradition bigger than themselves have figured that out.

Tired of decorating their life with bouquets of their own choosing, they are ready to go deeper, and even ready to put in the work that it requires. Because being a part of a religious tradition takes work.

Part of the nature of religion is that it delivers a message that is like sandpaper against our culture of narcissism. It's not all about you. And no, you can't make this stuff up.

Atheists say, yes, I can make this stuff up, that all religion and spirituality are made up. When we invent our own spirituality, with a flower from here and another from there, it is made up. But religious traditions created over time are bigger than anything you could do by yourself. And they are not like a prix fixe "pick two from column A, two from column B" menu.

It's easy to play by the rules of a religion in which you write your own script. Much harder to find meaning in the words of a book we did not write for ourselves, from a very different time.

It's easy to create God in your own image and then follow her. Much harder to work with the God who created you and did not seek your input at your own creation.

Anyone can find God alone on a picturesque mountaintop. The miracle is that we can find God in the company of other people as annoying as we are.

The fear of being judged judgmental

In response to my writing, I learned that some SBNRs took issue when I suggested that it is religious people who are on the fringe and cutting edge these days. It is profoundly countercultural to take an hour a week to worship something other than oneself. It's even weirder to do it with other people in community and over time, in a tradition older and larger than you are.

But other than being surprised by their own growing numbers, I found that most SBNRs were pretty open to my making a case it made for religious community.

But there were other readers who found my writing judgmental and even dangerous. They sent me countless e-mails telling me that I was a judgmental Christian who was giving the rest of Christianity a bad name. And who were these watchdogs? They were liberal mainline Protestants, who came from the same churches that I had been raised in and served as a pastor in myself. They were upset that I had made a case for attending churches like ours, or any church for that matter, lest I appear judgmental. Did they feel personally attacked? No, they felt outrage on behalf of those they felt were being judged.

This was their logic: Christians, who are by definition judgmental, deluded hypocrites responsible for most of the conflict in the world, are supposed to be nonjudgmental. "You, Lillian Daniel, were judgmental in your piece because you are a Christian, which is why people hate Christians. Which is why people hate us. And we were just about to get all these Christian haters back into our churches when you made us look judgmental by claiming that any of this matters."

My response was, "Dear nonjudgmental reader, if I am this judgmental as a follower of Jesus, just imagine how out of control I would be without him?" That didn't seem to help.

So some of my own people, liberal Christians, were furious with me for making a case for religion, even when it was a case that made room for all religions as well as no religion. What they seemed to hold true was the belief that making the case for religious community was de facto offensive to SBNRs. They believed that if we just listen compassionately to SBNRs, whatever they say about religion, these SBNRs will make their way into our churches and potluck suppers.

But apparently I had blown the chances of attracting SBNRs, by writing to an audience outside the confines of the church. *Those SBNRs drive us all crazy*, they seemed to be saying, *but you can't tell them that*. By saying that Christian community actually matters, by putting in print that I think it is more edifying than sitting alone looking for God in a coffee cup, I had played into SBNRs' assumptions that we are hostile, narrow-minded, mean-spirited, and judgmental.

These people of faith believed that the best way to get someone to join you is not to say anything critical of anyone. And it's probably better not to say anything positive about your own project of Christian community, because that would imply it might be better than being SBNR.

Instead, you should just exude niceness to people when

they criticize Christianity with uninformed, blanket state-ments. And if you apologize over and again for a church you are not a member of, they will finally realize you are different and they will come to your church. Given the shrinkage in churches over the last fifty years, this strategy doesn't seem to be working.

Of course, churches are full of the spiritual but not reli-gious and have been for quite some time because Ameri-can society is full of them. Some are those attend worship solely on the high holy days, like Christmas and Easter, hence the nickname "C.+E. Christians."

Churches are also populated by folks who are recov-ering from one form of Christianity or another. In many cases believers are truly happy to have found a new church but they don't want to spread the word. Why is that? Maybe they've been appalled by those "invitations" in the past, when someone knocked on their door or stopped them downtown to tell them Jesus loved them so much that if they didn't go to the right church, they would burn in hell. If that's what invitations come with, better not to invite anyone.

Maybe they are embarrassed by what passes on televi-sion and in political campaigns for Christianity. So they duck aside, not wanting to be associated with it.

Whatever the case, they have decided that the best pol-icy for open-minded Christians is, "Don't ask, don't tell." Stay in the closet. Don't share your faith.

But open-minded Christians have faith journeys that

are reasonable, rigorous and real. That's worth sharing. It's time for those Christians to stop apologizing and realize that *how we talk* about Christian community really matters. It matters to God, to the health of our churches, and to those in conversation with us. I wrote this book to spur us all into a more interesting conversation.

Chapter 4

The New Atheists Are
Old News

I N 2015, A PEW RESEARCH Center study on religious
participation in America confirmed what many of us
already knew: These days, when asked what their religion
is, one out of five people checks off "None." And for those
under the age of thirty, that number rises to one in three.
The widely circulated report "America's Changing Religious Landscape" introduced the "Nones," a category that
includes people who self-identify as atheists or agnostics, as
well as those who say their religion is "nothing in particular." The Nones now make up 23 percent of all U.S. adults,
up from 16 percent in 2007.

The big news was that the largest-growing group in the

country is a group of people who say they have no religious affiliation whatsoever. After the survey gained media attention, we had a new name for them: the "Nones," now as present in the religious conversation as the SBNRs. But were the Nones the same category as the SBNRs? Maybe, but not exactly.

There is more to the story. To begin with, this group is not uniformly nonreligious. Most of them say they believe in God, and about a third say religion is at least somewhat important in their lives.

Nones and the new atheists

So clearly, some of the Nones are SBNRs, interested in and experiencing the divine but not part of a religious community, hence their willingness to check off "None."

But Nones in the survey also represent a group that is larger than the SBNRs. Surely many of them do not believe in God, and do so without apology. This was no surprise, as the "new atheists" were gaining media and cultural attention, with books claiming the title "atheist," and often denigrating all religious life. This was the new acceptable prejudice being put forth in bestselling books such as Christopher Hitchens's *God Is Not Great* and *The Portable Atheist*, and Richard Dawkins's *The God Delusion*, and increasingly finding its way into everyday conversation. Observing such authors and other public personas

acceptable prejudice

like entertainer Bill Maher, I found the debate and conversation at first refreshing. I am all in favor of religious freedom, satire, and debate.

But it soon grew tedious. They were angry and came out swinging. I think they were tired of being the butt end of jokes, or forced into silence. But they were slinging stereotypes. The churches and religious communities they parodied bore little resemblance to the ones I had seen, and I was pretty sure they were aware of that, too.

Admittedly, in debate we often take a straw man, setting up an extreme example in order to make a point. That was what I had done with my short "Stop Boring Me" piece in the *Huffington Post* and the composite character of the "sunset person."

But there was a difference, I thought. It's one thing to tell your straw men to stop boring you, because they are not as unique as they want to be. It's another to claim that your straw man is responsible for all the wars in human history, or to claim that your straw man spews hate and venom at every turn, predicting hellfire and damnation for everyone outside the straw man club.

Atheist adman

In a manner that was surprising to some, Ron Reagan, the son of President Ronald Reagan, made this 2015 television ad for the Freedom from Religion Foundation:

"Hi, I'm Ron Reagan, an unabashed atheist, and I'm alarmed by the intrusion of religion into our secular government. That's why I'm asking you to support the Freedom from Religion Foundation, the nation's largest and most effective association of atheists and agnostics, working to keep state and church separate, just like our Founding Fathers intended. Please support the Freedom from Religion Foundation. Ron Reagan, lifelong atheist, not afraid of burning in hell."

Initially the three major networks, ABC, NBC, and CBS, refused the 30-second spot, but it aired successfully on CNN, and the "sign-off" got most of the attention. It was witty, unexpected, but it also plays to an assumption about Christians and people of faith. It assumes we all think Ron Reagan is going to burn in hell for not believing in God.

Personally, I think he's already been there, what with his tortuous relationship with his father and a hard life of public scrutiny and not being able to be himself. But blame that on the fishbowl of the White House, or a nationally beloved dad who was as uninterested in his son's spiritual beliefs as he was in his ballet career.

Nice neighborhood atheists

My hunch is that most atheists in the None category are not like Hitchens, or Maher. I suspect they are like most atheists I know personally, who tend to be a heady, ethical, self-reflective bunch. The atheists I know are often consciously community minded and careful not to offer sweeping generalizations of religious people, because they know what it feels like to be on the other end of that. For much of human history, atheists were branded as morally lacking, evil, irredeemable. These were unfair accusations that they for the most part did not throw at others, at least in my personal experience.

And of course, many atheists when pressed will tell you that they are agnostic. It's not so much that they are certain that God does not exist. Rather, they admit they don't know. That's an agnostic.

The fact that atheists and agnostics have to delineate themselves to death in terms of belief is part of that larger problem in American Christianity. Fundamentalist Christians brought us the belief obsession—not the atheists, and not the rest of Christianity either. And yet we all get caught up in the same unhelpful fundamentalist literalism that privileges belief over all other aspects of religious life. Hence the atheist is forced into silence or a defensive posture, neither of which is any way to live. And now, I think open-minded religious people feel the same way, silenced. The trouble is, when one group is silent, the louder Fundamentalists get to define religion.

Which in turn keeps many intelligent and thoughtful people away, trying to figure out which category of non-believer they are, in order to explain themselves to their belief-obsessed Christian friends.

Responding to the rising number of Nones

We have to break the cycle. Silence and apologizing are not the answer. We have to give voice to the many people who love God in a specific community but don't believe heaven has seats that are reserved only for them. And when I say "we," I mean ordinary people, not the heads of religions or denominational leaders. We can't wait for them to do it. We know from experience they don't do that thing well.

For example, at the time of the Pew study about the rising numbers of Nones, various Christian leaders were asked to comment on the report and finally got a little airtime. It was a big moment for the previously undercherished mainline Protestant, Catholic, and Evangelical leaders, who finally got asked for their opinion when invited to respond to the survey results in various news outlets. For the most part, their responses were unedifying. "What's wrong with these Nones? Why aren't they joining the church?" many asked. When it was pointed out that if you're under thirty, there's a one in three chance that you're a None, the religious leaders responded with predictable blame casting: "What's wrong with the young people? What's wrong with their parents? Why didn't they ask the coach to cancel Sunday practice? Maybe there's still time for us to go meet with the coach. Let's fix this."

This is why the Nones don't like us

I felt embarrassed by the church spokespersons' responses to the survey on a couple of levels. First, the fact that any of these leaders expressed shock or surprise was shocking and surprising. Had they not been to their own churches lately? Did they not notice who was missing?

Second, their criticism of the culture rang false. Suddenly, even churches that were open and liberal were fussing like the cranky "church lady" from the old *Saturday Night Live*. What a terrible society we must be, to produce such growing numbers of Nones. Did none of these leaders think that freedom of choice was a good thing and that honest self-expression was healthy? Both for the church as well as society?

You'd think that as followers of Jesus, we in the church would be able to roll with the news that we were no longer the center of the cultural universe. Given our founder's place in society, you would think we'd be okay there, or at least willing to check ourselves before panicking. But instead, the liberal Christians aging out of denominational leadership hearkened back to some folksy apple pie all-church ice cream social past. Catholics waxed vaguely about attracting the young people with "upbeat music." And the Evangelicals who already had that so-called "upbeat music" admitted it wasn't working so well for them anymore either. (As a side note, it might just be time to stop calling the music of the baby boomers "contemporary.")

This could be good news

In response to the survey about the rise of the Nones, I wanted to hear a few religious leaders say what I was feeling: that this could be good news, for religious freedom and for religious community. I wanted to hear that for centuries the church has gotten fat and spoiled and too used to getting its own way. We now had an opportunity to face reality, face each other, and get lean. What was it that we wanted to share that was worth sharing? Not our inflated budgets and our anxiety about funding them, I hope. Not our overly large buildings that were constructed by human hands, hearts, and egos, just like other buildings. Not one style of music over another, because here's a news flash: People can get their music anywhere. Not our anxiety about our shrinking place in society. You can get that at the Masonic lodge, the union hall, and the organ performance department of any university that still has an organ performance department. So let's not compete with other dying organizations. This is an opportunity for us to share what we have, not what we are stuck with and don't want anymore ourselves.

Outsiders? It's the Bible's sweet spot

I also wanted someone to point out that being a smaller, outsider group was our sweet spot, as Christians. And that we had plenty of guidance about how to live like that, not from recent church growth literature or seminars, but from the Bible itself.

Most of the Bible was written from the perspective of outsiders trying to follow a countercultural religion. So we're not alone here. If we need help with this state of affairs, we already have thousands of years of reflection from a community larger, older, and perhaps wiser than we are in this tiny slice of time we call our own.

But instead, church leaders weighed in with criticism and panic at the news that we Christians were farther off to the sidelines than we thought. Many obviously missed and reminisced for the days of Christendom when they had an automatic market share. Even worse, some seemed, just now, to be learning that things had changed. And worst of all, it was these leaders who wanted to tell the rest of us to fix it. For the most part, these leaders were on their way out. After passing go and picking up their retirement check, they wanted to let the next generation know how bad it had gotten. How did they know? A survey had told them. The news was bad. We have to grow. You guys need to fix it.

Ranging from criticism of the Nones to panic about its own institutional survival, the church's whining media response said it all. If you lined up all the church responders, you could see exactly why being a None outside of this community was more appealing than being one of them.

The Nones have always been with us

The Nones are really not a new group. We've had them all along. Maybe in the old days, they came to the Second Presbyterian Church on Christmas and Easter. And, gosh darn it, their grandbaby is going to be baptized here, too, and their kids are going to get married here, but you won't see them other than that.

There's an old joke about one minister telling another how to get rid of all the bats in the church belfry. "Put the bats through confirmation class," the pastor says. "After confirmation, you'll never see them again."

A decade ago, the Nones would probably have ticked off "Presbyterian" on a survey but now they can tell the truth. People are just more comfortable self-identifying as *Nones* today.

There's another corny joke about this pastor who's looking out at the Christmas crowd. He sees all of these people he doesn't recognize and says, "You people only come on Christmas and Easter. You need to be warriors for the Lord." Afterward, one of these people shakes the pastor's hand and says, "Pastor, I *am* a warrior for the Lord; it's just that I'm in the secret service."

Chapter 5

The Four Types of Nones

MY THEORY ABOUT THE NONES is that, as usual, the church is about twenty years behind what's happening in culture. We're still trying to talk to the Nones as though they are ticked off at some *other* type of Christianity and just haven't heard about whatever flavor we are. That may be one segment of Nones but it's a shrinking segment.

The Nones, like any religious group, are a varied mix of people with many segments. For the sake of clarity, I find four groups that I encounter as Nones. There are the "No Longers," who were once in the church, but are no longer in the church. They may come back, but there is another group that was once there but does not want to come back, the "No Ways." They may be mad, hurt, or simply analytical, but they are clear they don't want or need it.

Unlike those two groups, there are two more who have not experienced any of it. They are the "Never Haves," who haven't thought about it before, and then there are the ones who are curious, whom I call the "Not Yets."

The Four Types of Nones

1. **No Way.** This person has made a deliberate and well-thought-out decision not to attend church, often in reaction to a genuine hurt.

2. **No Longer.** This person used to attend church, but doesn't anymore and doesn't particularly miss it.

3. **Never Have.** This person has never experienced church, and may be the grown child of parents in one of the first two groups.

4. **Not Yet.** These people may be curious about church and may choose to show up. Often, the church treats them like one of the first two groups.

Listening to the No Ways

Much of the apologizing that I am tired of doing was directed toward No Ways.

It was exhausting because often their grievances with religion were real and heartbreaking. To picture the No

Ways, just think about all the people who have given up on church as a result of the Catholic sexual abuse scandals.

But remarkably, many of those No Ways still end up finding another church, and against all odds, they try again. They must be pretty passionate about religious community to do that. I've heard their stories, and they inspire me.

In fact, the churches I have pastored attracted No Ways. In some cases we were able to show them another way of being in the church that did not feel like what they had experienced before. We had women clergy. We could perform their gay weddings. They could trust that their children would have their deepest values of inclusivity upheld by a Jesus-following church that believed Jesus would have included everybody, too.

But sometimes No Ways really mean No Way and they want to stay that way. I think that's fine. If you respect religious freedom, you have to respect the freedom to choose no religion. This is why some people call the Nones "Dones." They are finished, No Way, in that moment. If they've been hurt or injured, who could blame them? Not I.

But what I hate to see is someone who isn't really choosing *no* religion, but is instead recovering from being hurt by *one experience* with religion. I think those people are worth listening to and talking to, and they deserve to know why religious community matters to the rest of us. The No Ways are not always Done.

Talking to the No Longers

As for the No Longers, I think they are a harder group to engage. The No Ways are passionate, at least. The No Longers have drifted. They may not have been that passionate to begin with. They probably don't remember making a big break with the church, but just gradually drifted away. There was no big event, at least at church, unless it was a life event like kids growing up and no longer being the reason the parents came to church. This group often will return to religious community at key life moments, such as weddings and more often funerals. They may come at Christmas and Easter.

With No Longers, the church people will often offer them utilitarian arguments, or small enticements to "check us out, we've changed." They might dangle the promise of a new pastor who really can preach, or a better music director or a larger choir. They may try to coax the No Longers into some leadership role, so that they will feel "more involved." I am against all these arguments, by the way, but especially the last one. The last thing a new pastor needs is a bunch of committee members who have long since determined that worship is irrelevant, but are still willing to come in order to voice an opinion at committee meetings. It's like the worst of all worlds for them and for the church—exposure to the worst of the institution without any of the inspiration.

But at their heart, the No Longers are wondering about purpose. They have lots of ways they can spend their time, and if they're not in church, they may well be doing "something more meaningful."

In general, they carry the religious values with them out into the world. They volunteer and contribute and get more out of that than church. The No Longers when pressed may tell you there was more to their drifting than simply drifting. They never consciously picked up their marbles and went home. They just stopped coming over to play.

When pressed, they often have a story of institutional frustration or administrative exhaustion. These are the last people you should be tempting back into the church with promises of a committee post. They know all about church committees. They need to be loved and fed, and somehow the church stopped being a place where they could get that.

When tragedy hits, they may return, and hopefully reconnect with God and God's imperfect people in a tradition bigger than themselves. These things seem more important at the hospital bedside of a parent, a grown child's tragedy, a heartbreaking diagnosis of one's own.

Times like that can open up the religious reserves that the No Longers built up with years of practice before leaving. They have that foundation and, hopefully, some community that wants to make up for being so irrelevant.

But what about the Never Haves and Not Yets?

People in churches have some idea how to talk to the No Ways and the No Longers, but not much of an idea how to talk to people who have never been a part of a religious community, the other fastest-growing group of Nones. They can relate to the No Longers and No Ways because they may be on the edge of those categories themselves, or remember being there. Much of the response to the Pew survey about the rising numbers of Nones came out of that conversation space. There was self-criticism, reference to being a "different kind of church," all of which might make sense to someone who had experienced church before. But almost none of the responses to the survey would have been compelling to the Never Haves and the Not Yets. In general, those are the people our institutional leaders are least equipped to talk to, because they still can't get their heads around the reality that, for these people, church is not even a reference point.

Curious Nones

Many of the Nones are curious and ask questions, but church people may not be the best listeners. We start apologizing before explaining. Or we start explaining without ever having listened. It's not that the Nones are not interested in God or religious community. A growing number of them are. They may not be ready to show up but I think they are ready to talk, to share, to learn and be heard. Is that too much for them to ask? Apparently it is, because many report they cannot find that kind of back and forth exchange, even in open-minded communities. Instead they get to listen in on the church's inside baseball. It's an internal conversation among those who are immersed in church, and I do not think the Nones are interested in that. Sometimes it feels like the church is in the business of answering questions that most Nones are not asking.

They want to know if you've experienced God, not what church committees you've served on. They want to know why people sing in church and who they think they are singing to, not why you chose your new music director and what style of music won your latest worship contests.

They want to know what a shared pursuit of faith feels like and how to get there, but they're not yet sold on its value—and they may never be. And while you may think religious community could add something, if the Nones had that specific a vacuum in their lives, they would have filled it already. Instead, they have a vague yearning for something, but very little yearning to hear an apology or a lecture about something they have yet to experience.

It's like making the case for baseball

Sometimes it helps to imagine the same conversation taking place about something else other than religion. Take baseball, for example.

I am not a baseball fan. I never have been and probably never will.

It doesn't make much sense to ask me something like this, with a worried but caring look in your eyes, "Lillian, does it worry you that you're not a baseball fan?"

"No."

"Well, you should try becoming a baseball fan."

"Why?"

"Baseball is amazing."

"No it isn't."

"Have you even been to a baseball game?"

"Yes."

"Well, what did you think?"

"It was boring."

"Ahhh...yes," the baseball fan responds with a knowing smile. "That's because you don't know much about it. Have you studied the rules? Learned to keep score? Memorized statistics?"

"No."

"Well, that's why you don't enjoy baseball!"

"Okay."

"So why haven't you spent more time learning about baseball, before deciding you don't like it?"

"Um, because I have other things to do."

"Well, you might want to take some time to do it."

"Why?"

If someone tries to convince me to have an interest in baseball, they're assuming I have some sense of the value of baseball. But maybe baseball has upset me in some way. You know, I lived in Chicago. Maybe I've been hurt by baseball. Maybe somebody paid too much attention to baseball and not to me.

Or maybe I feel that baseball is responsible for all of the wars that have ever happened in human history because baseball lovers are so narrow-minded. I don't have any sense of the intrinsic worth of baseball, nor do I believe my life will be improved by going to a baseball game, and you're telling me, "You don't really know enough about baseball. There are lots of different teams out there!" I say, "Who cares?"

If I've been to a baseball game and I've loved baseball and now I'm upset about it, you can reach me. But if I don't know what it is and I don't miss it, that approach is not going to work. So the question is this: How do you talk about baseball to somebody who does not care about it and does not feel they are missing anything?

Stop apologizing and listen

That's how the Never Haves feel about church. This new generation of Nones, the Never Haves and Not Yets, include many who have never experienced any religious community. And they're in a very different place from the angry refugees who fled religious community. They may be open, wanting to learn—they just haven't done it yet.

To reach this group of Nones, we'll have to stop answering questions that are not being asked. We'll have to stop assuming that people are angry with the church or disillusioned with the church. Because a growing group of the Nones are totally unfamiliar with the church.

These people have not yet been hurt by the church. (Give us time; we'll get to you!) But for now, consider how strange it would be to see a group of people engaging together, only to have your polite questions answered by a string of apologies and defensiveness.

No one should be made to feel stupid in a conversation, which means we strike a balance between challenging each other and listening. This conversation should be as good for the religious person as it is for the None. Both should come out ahead, both learning. And as to which group needs this the most, I think it could be the church people. The rise of the Nones clarifies things, forces a rethinking.

Actually talking to this group of Nones, listening to their dreams and visions, their worries and needs, may remind us why we do all this. The Nones and the conversations they inspire may save the church.

They're not all mad at the church...yet

In the generation of people under thirty, one out of three is a None. They are likely to be Never Haves and Not Yets, raised by No Way or No Longer parents who left the church and did not raise their children religiously. Sometimes these parents will say, "Religion was forced on me so I wanted to let my children choose for themselves."

This is like saying you want your kids to choose their own favorite literature in adulthood by not teaching them to read as children. It's hard to choose any one great genre of literature when you've never read a serious book with anyone in community or over time.

But those parents, that first wave of Nones, may have been injured by the church or bored by the church or let down by the church. Unlike their children, they have some idea in their head of what church is because they are No Ways and No Longers. You may convince them that your church is what they've wanted all along, because at least you can tell them why it's different from some other church. They have a point of reference that their children do not have. As usual, the church is about twenty years behind what's happening. We're still trying to talk to the Nones as though they are all ticked off at some other type of Christianity and just haven't heard about our brand yet. But more and more of the Nones don't know about brands. They have no other brand experience to compare to. They're asking about baseball because they have never seen a baseball game, while the church responds as if its job is to convince a Cubs fan to follow the White Sox.

Chapter 6

Raised without Religion, Choosing Church

INCREASINGLY, WE'RE GOING TO SEE people with no church background, who are curious. As much as church leaders bemoan their absence, I can tell you as a pastor that they do show up in church, where their deep questions get met with equivocating. They are baffled by all the apologizing for injuries they have not experienced at our hands.

Despite all that, they sometimes stay, and when they do, they can get pretty excited about this new thing called church or religious community. They want to hear about a tradition that is bigger than they are. They are relieved to discover they are not the first ones to notice that bad things happen to good people. They're smart people who always suspected that there had to be more to theology than having your wishes granted by a magical genie God. They are ready to read voraciously about all the different approaches to the problem of suffering and evil, which have been going on for generations. They might even come to love the book of Job once they have slogged through all the pithy responses Job's friends give him and perhaps seen some of their own in there. By the time they get to the ending, and learn that suffering is a mystery but not God's punishment, they might even claim Job as their favorite book of the Bible. But they want to be introduced to the treasures of the theological world, not directed away from every bad moment of church history. We should say, "Yes! Read the rabbis, read Jesus as someone who read the writings of rabbis. Then, you'll be prepared to criticize the Crusades as someone who has thought about these things deeply and knows that any war for souls, sovereignty, and slavery that claims to be Christian is not what it claims to be. People of faith have been standing up to each other on those matters for thousands of years, pushing and pulling each other back to a core message of God's love, which sharpens and corrects the church, with reforms, mystical revelations, brave acts, and courageous stands. And none of it would have happened if we'd all just sat by ourselves looking for God in the sunset, or simply read the Bible alone somewhere."

It's not just the Nones who need reminding

Contrary to the oft-told story of the decline of various religious traditions, I can tell you that there are still people who were raised in a tradition that they still appreciate and have decided to stick with. Whatever we say to the None or the newcomer will not be wasted on the longtime church attender. They need to hear it, too.

In today's religious landscape of unlimited choice, these people can sometimes feel a little embarrassed about being so boring. They keep sheepishly quiet amid the loud debates about how awful religion is, afraid to admit they've been pretty blessed. They don't want to look like they've been asleep at the wheel and missed something.

These long-term churchgoers are a little like the first-time visitors or Nones. They want someone to make a case for why all this matters, because they're not sure how to do it themselves without being jerks. They show up for worship, as they have come for thousands of years, a mixed bag of mutts and strays, seeking some divine connection in worship.

Is your religious community ready for all that? Are you ready for the long-term Cubs fan to sit next to someone who has never seen a baseball game before? That's the beauty of worshipping something larger than ourselves, in community and over time. There's room under that big tent, when we remember that we are not there to worship ourselves, our team, or even the sport, but rather the God who created us all.

When Nones come to church

When talk about religion is hostile or nonexistent, the whole freight and weight of this conversation gets shifted to places of worship. Just as school systems now carry social service loads that far outweigh their old task of education, so weekly worship has become the place where everything lands. There is no Head Start or pre-K class; everyone shows up at every level to talk about God. But given how stagnant worship can be, it has become an invisible and one-way conversation for the anonymous seeker. When Nones come to church, they do not wear a sign or special uniform announcing who they are and where they come from. They look just like someone else there. So it has become more important than ever to clarify who—and why—we are worshipping.

Church leaders spend lots of time dreaming up worship services for the Nones, and some have done a terrific job of meeting people where they are with specific worship services targeted to one group or another. Megachurches met the needs of suburban seekers but this was nothing new. Ethnic parishes met the needs of new immigrants. There have always been seeker-friendly services. What is new is the realm of choices people have today. There is no one clear entry point. But the good and bad news is that the

Nones don't always look for None-friendly worship; they just show up whether we're ready or not.

Yes, there are churches that have devoted themselves to the seeker and the newcomer, but in general, those churches grow because someone invites the seeker, who may well be a No Way or No Longer, open to some fresh new vision of church.

The Never Haves and Not Yets would probably think that having a worship service just for them was weird. After all, aren't we all supposed to be worshipping God? And in a society in which you don't have to attend church, wouldn't a truly new person be turned off by pandering entertainment addressed to their parents, the baby boomers?

Many Nones are indeed put off by arena entertainment. They are open to and drawn to mystery. But they don't want it to be too mysterious as in: It is a mystery what page we are singing from and when we are supposed to sit and stand. Let God be mysterious. Let your worship be welcoming.

That's poor communication, not divine mystery

And when newcomers think the greatest mystery is whether or not they are welcome, that's just plain bad.

So trust me, after leading four very different churches and witnessing growth for a variety of reasons, I can tell you this. Just as Nones show up at church unidentified, some churchgoers are similarly unidentified—and they are about to be Nones. They are on their way out. It all depends on what we convey in worship. Does any of this matter? Do we worship as if we think God is really listening? Do we explain why we do things? Because hopefully these things we do in worship matter and the new people matter to us as well.

Too many religious communities conduct worship as if visitors were as rare as unicorns.

"We don't need to print the Lord's Prayer, because everyone here knows it!" they say.

That's like saying, "We don't need a salt lick at the end of the rainbow because unicorns don't exist."

But Nones do exist and they do sometimes come to church. They may come once, but they come, and everything we do ought to include the possibility that it's not a show we put on for one another, but a powerful connection between humanity and God that it is better when we do it together.

And the first-time worship visitor is not going to your Bible study, no matter how much you think they'd learn there. They'll learn it first in a church service whether you mean to be teaching something or not. So no matter what your religious community is, you had better start teaching things as part of worship, in a way that includes intelligent, curious Nones who may stop by that day. You can say that people should learn these things in a new member class or Bible study, but worship is the church's front door, and if the house is a mysterious mess, they won't come back.

So let's conduct ourselves in worship as if God is listening, and as if a total stranger is always looking in to learn about God, too.

Nones don't wear name tags

Asking visitors to announce themselves signals the rarity of the occasion. Asking them to embarrass themselves by wearing a name tag is even worse. It is the self-centered church that wants the newcomer to make the job of being welcoming easier for those who are already there. Very few Nones want to do that. They'll just slip in and out again.

It's one of the reasons "Visitor" name tags don't work. Who wants to label themselves a visitor? Hell is a place where first-time visitors get a name tag, because the old-timers are too selfish to wear them.

In church it ought to be the opposite. The old-timers should wear the name tags, to show that they are the ones extending themselves to the newcomer. But sadly, members seldom do. "We all know each other. Why, everyone knows me!" They think that not wearing a name tag and not having to meet any new people are perks of membership, like sitting in the back pew when the whole church is empty. Membership has its privileges, like rubbing nonmembers' noses in their lack of belonging until they decide to become members, who can then refuse to wear a name tag, too.

The only time this bizarre behavior works is when you are selling membership in something people already think they need, like front-row seats at their favorite show. It does not work when you are selling season baseball tickets to someone like me who has no interest in baseball. And if for some reason, I do end up at a Cubs game, please don't ask me to wear a "Visitor/I've never liked baseball before" name tag. It's like throwing chum in the water. Particularly with Cubs fans.

Probably the most important thing to remember with this group is that our worship needs to make sense to them. That doesn't mean dumbing it down, but it does mean constantly teaching. If you're going to say the Lord's Prayer, explain what it is and define the words. Don't throw words like "trespasses" out there and leave the Never Haves guessing what it means. You'll only succeed in making them feel like they don't belong.

As welcoming as the opening scene of a horror movie

Sometimes we alienate the Never Haves and Not Yets at the moment we think we are being most welcoming. Someone makes an announcement that tells attendees to "see Pastor about joining the Kitchen Chix downstairs in Pilgrim Hall" or "sign up with Mary at coffee hour for Hymns and Belles." What is coffee hour? What if you don't know what time of day this weird religious group drinks its coffee? (Apparently this weird cult limits all coffee intake to a single hour.)

What if you don't know Pastor? She sounds awfully busy seeing people about events. As for "downstairs in Pilgrim Hall," it took all your courage to come to church this morning. You're not ready for Pilgrim Hall, even if they do tell you just to follow the crowd into the basement. It's as inviting as the first scene in a horror movie. The newcomer thinks, "I'm the only person here who doesn't know who Pastor is or any of these other things. The groups all seem to be aligned along the lines or gender identity or animal species, and they all partake of coffee at the same hour in a hall named after the witch burners. I must not belong here."

And later, if you tell people you visited their church but didn't return, they'll criticize you for not going to coffee hour or joining a committee, since that's where you really get to know people. Which, of course, is only true of the people who already know each other.

Answering questions the Nones are not asking

So how do we decode our conversation so it's not just among ourselves? How do we make it a conversation that works for the person coming in without any frame of reference? And why does it matter?

It matters not because we want to build our institutions but because worship better prepares us to serve our Loving Creator in the world. Through worship we prepare people to experience the divine, to do the divine will, to create good and beauty and truth, and to live life abundantly. To do that in today's culture, we have to have a generous spirit about the really weird ways God works.

No matter which group of Nones we are reaching out to, it's time to stop defining ourselves by what we are not, and learn to describe ourselves as who, and whose, we really are.

What's happening is that the church is becoming the church again. At our best, we've always cared the most about the outsider. Maybe talking to the Nones will remind us who we are. After all, every religion was once, at its inception, just a weird gathering of people who had never done this religion thing before. At some point, they chose it, and invited others to choose it, too. Come join us in this God thing. It's better if we do it together, but it won't be easier. We're all too different to make it easy. We're a mixed bag. But come join this mixed bag of nuts. We don't have any cashews yet, and the mix could be better because of you.

A mixed bag of nuts

The Nones are not homogenous. Just like religious people, the Nones are also a mixed bag of nuts. And of the four

ies—the No Longer, the No Way, the Never Have, and the Not Yet—it's the first two, the No Longer and the No Way, who have had most of our attention in the mainline church. The church can act like a terrible teacher who only responds to the loudest and angriest kid, ignoring the quiet ones with the good questions. They just look on and listen in from the sidelines, confused at the teacher's antics.

We've engaged those two loud groups over doctrine and polity, defining ourselves by what we are not. "We're not like this Christian. We're not like that. We ordain women. We'll perform your gay marriage."

We've done plenty of that and it may work for people who have said "no way" to some other church, or just drifted away and said "no longer." But what about the others?

The Never Haves and the Not Yets are not asking those questions, and we never hear them ask anything out loud when we're doing all the talking. So they just show up and listen in on an internecine debate among religious people, many of whom are on their way out. What if instead we geared it all toward the ones at the back of church, either leaning in or drifting out? That's the group we have to really think about in our worship as we consider why it matters. What can we do when they get here? What can we do as they consider their way out?

We have to have worship that makes sense to them. It doesn't mean dumbing it down, but it means constantly teaching, and including. It's not just the first-time visitor who thinks, "Everybody knows what this means, but I have no idea." The long-term member and the Not Yets may both be thinking, "This feels like a club and I'm not comfortable or welcome here."

Are Nones religious?

What makes a person religious? I look to the root of the word "religious," which is "community." So anyone can participate in religious community and be religious.

But if your definition is about personal belief, then you might make a statement that the Nones are increasingly "less religious." The Pew study clearly defines religion as belief of some kind, when it talks about the nonreligiosity of the nonreligious:

> At the same time, between the Pew Research Center's two Religious Landscape Studies—conducted in 2007 and 2014—we also see consistent evidence that the "Nones" are becoming *less* religious. For example, the share of religious "Nones" who say they believe in God, while still a majority, has fallen from 70 to 61 percent over that seven-year period. Only 27 percent of "Nones" are absolutely certain about God's existence, down from 36 percent in 2007. And fully a third of religiously unaffiliated Americans (33 percent) now say they do *not* believe in God, up 11 percentage points over that time.

The Pew study provides an example of how the institutional religious world is asking and answering questions the Nones are not asking. They look for a cause for the "less religious" nature of the Nones.

The question of *why* the Nones are growing less religious in terms of belief does not have a simple answer. But just as is the case for why Nones are growing as a share of the U.S. public, generational replacement appears to be playing a role. Religiously unaffiliated Americans are younger, on average, than the general public to begin with, and the youngest adults in the group—that is, those who have entered adulthood in the last several years—are even less religious than "Nones" overall.

To me, the answer is not mysterious. People who do not participate in religious community care less about religious community. They are not exposed to it. If they do not see the value of it, where or how can they be expected to learn about its practices? To be surprised that nonreligious people are less likely to pray is like being surprised that vegetarians eat less and less meat.

The Pew research made the point that fully seven in ten of the youngest millennials (born between 1990 and 1996) with no religious affiliation say religion is not important in their lives. A similar share (70 percent) also say they seldom or never pray, and 42 percent say they do not believe in God, all bigger percentages than among religious "Nones" as a whole.

Again, where is the surprise in this? Why would it be

important to their lives? And surely there should be no judgment attached to that. It is sensible and reasonable.

Far stranger to me are the statistics about how many Americans believe they are religious but do not attend worship in any community.

But when that is reversed in the case of the Never Haves, it makes sense to me. Their experience of God and prayer come from a lack of exposure, and so it is not a felt absence.

What I have learned is that, unlike the No Ways, many of the Never Haves and Not Yets are clear on what they currently do or do not do. They are comfortable admitting where they are today and they may be very open to doing something different in the future. So what's stopping them?

Perception problem

A 2007 study by the Barna group explored twenty specific images related to Christianity, including ten favorable and ten unfavorable perceptions. Among young non-Christians, nine out of the top twelve perceptions were negative. Common negative perceptions include that present-day Christianity is judgmental (87 percent), hypocritical (85 percent), old-fashioned (78 percent), and too involved in politics (75 percent).

Even among young people within the church, two strong negative perceptions have been growing. The first is that the church is overly political and inappropriately wrapped up in right-wing politics.

And the second clear negative: Present-day Christianity is "antihomosexual." When asked more in-depth questions, the young people revealed that this was more than a perception of an institutional stance. They felt it ran through Christian people, perceiving that Christians show excessive contempt and unloving attitudes toward gays and lesbians. One of the most frequent criticisms of young Christians was that they believe the church has made homosexuality a "bigger sin" than anything else.

This Barna study confirmed what I was afraid of when I read eighth grade confirmation papers in my church in the suburbs of Chicago. Christianity has a huge perception problem. Even these children, raised in an open-minded church, took on the media's portrayal of a rigid and judgmental church. Is it any surprise that young people with no exposure to anything different would take it on as well?

Since 2007, the movement for gay marriage has included visible support from churches like my own. I'd like to think those perceptions have changed but consider when the young people were raised and by whom.

Their parents experienced the rise of the religious right, and either supported it, or turned away from the church because of it. But either way, their children, now young adults, were shaped by their parents' choices and that time in American church history.

Of those who stayed and were a part of the religious

right, their children experienced a highly politicized version of Christianity that was increasingly at odds with their
diversity-friendly social milieu. For these young Christians,
and non-Christians, the LGBTQ community was not theo-
retical or out there, but increasingly right here and perhaps
they were members of it themselves.

Raised without religion, choosing church

For those whose parents left the church, and became No
Ways or No Longers, many of those young people were
raised without religion. Perhaps their parents wanted them
to choose for themselves, a common perspective among
adults who have left a religion they felt was oppressive.

But as a child of that generation myself, I am all too
familiar with the stance of parents who want their children to choose the type of literature they prefer, but don't
ever teach their children to read. While I was raised in
church, most of my friends at college were not, and they
had already determined not to raise their children in any
organized religion.

I was a Bible study dropout

So what about someone like me, an odd anomaly amid all
these studies? I was raised in a relaxed and loving church

environment by parents who supported the human and civil rights of all people. When I got to college, I was surprised to attend Christian groups and discover that they were homophobic. Naturally, I knew Christians could be that way, but I didn't think that in college, they'd all be that way. I didn't recognize that theology or their culture. As I look back, as a college student in the Reagan years, conservative Christians were the only ones having college Bible studies. Liberal Christians like me were studying Zen Buddhism, majoring in church history, and considering careers as academics because whatever God practice was happening at college bore no relationship to anything I wanted to do. That became my story.

I was one of those "don't ask, don't tell" Christians who didn't want to be associated with those other, louder Christians on TV. I was discovering feminism, gay rights, and I was riding the crest of the politically correct wave, back when "politically correct" wasn't even a pejorative term, but something self-referentially witty.

In college, we thought we were enlightened and making progress as human beings. Most of my peers saw religion as something to be left behind, like superstition, patriarchy, and slavery. And I wanted to agree about the human progress part. Nothing in those weird college Bible study groups seemed to fit with progress. Instead they seemed to be hearkening backward to a more brutal time. I stopped going.

Being a religion major was a great way to duck both groups, the conservative Christians and the liberal antireligionists. That's where I hid out, in a closet marked "Religious Studies."

Saints and freedom fighters

I got to study medieval Christian mysticism, which meant a little rubbed off on me, as I read the beautiful prayers and images of Saint Teresa of Avila, the subject of my college thesis. The antireligion people considered studying a medieval mystical nun to be okay, provided one considered one's historical subjects feminist lesbians whose history needed to be uncovered by modern research.

But I was reading Teresa of Avila for who she really was and claimed to be, a follower of Jesus who had dark nights of the soul where her despair was so desolate and dark it threatened to kill her. In her crazed thirst for God and meaning, I saw myself. She languished at the edges of an unfair and sexist world, afraid to be exposed for her family's ancient Jewish roots. She was a reformer in a Catholic Church which was reeling from righteous attacks by Protestant reformers, but also trying to reform itself.

In college, I studied modern-day Liberation theologians from around the world who stood at the side of the oppressed. There was Gustavo Gutierrez, who said, "The God of Exodus is the God of history and of political liberation more than he is the God of nature."

I was raised overseas in former British colonies and then

in London. In the Church of England, I had never heard anything like Gutierrez before, saying, "The denunciation of injustice implies the rejection of the use of Christianity to legitimize the established order." Suffice it to say, this kind of theology was not standard fare during the homilies at the Anglican church of my ex-patriot upbringing.

Nor was any of it familiar to me from Sunday mornings with my extended family back in South Carolina. The voice of black theology made me see things differently. I agreed with James Cone, who said, "The Gospel of liberation is bad news to all oppressors because they have defined their freedom in terms of slavery of others."

But I was still a Christian and so was he. I was discovering whole new worlds and new worlds within old ones. The subject of my study, Saint Teresa of Avila, was a medieval political hell-raiser who fought for the same liberation in her own context and time.

In the complexity of Teresa's world, I saw the complexity of my own, the brokenness of human institutions and the brokenness of my own young and hopeful heart. Her book, *The Interior Castle*, was more life changing to me than any political doctrine I might use to analyze it. My growing feminism was drawn to her mysticism and political savvy. My growing doubts found their rest in the dark nights of the soul she so honestly wrote about, as I explored my own Interior Castle in search of God. She saw and experienced the love of Jesus in her soul, and I wanted to do it, too.

Who among us has never been a None? Teresa of Avila, who became a nun of the Counter-Reformation, was the consummate None herself when she was young.

At some point, she chose monastic religious community, with all its constraints, and then dug in deeply. She changed her church and, generations later, she continues to change the church, by changing readers like me. I became what she could not become, an ordained minister who presides at the communion table.

And she remains what I am not, a mystical medieval nun whose words cross the centuries in their crisp articulation of the mysterious path that somehow we can share. "It is foolish to think that we will enter heaven without entering into ourselves."

Part II

RELIGION WITHOUT RANTING

Our hearts are restless until they find their rest in thee.   AUGUSTINE OF HIPPO, 354–430

All I have seen teaches me to trust the Creator for all I have not seen.

RALPH WALDO EMERSON, 1803–1882

"I believe in God, only I spell it Nature."

FRANK LLOYD WRIGHT, 1867–1959

Science without religion is lame, religion without science is blind.

ALBERT EINSTEIN, 1879–1955

Certain new theologians dispute original sin, which is the only part of Christian theology which can really be proved.

G. K. CHESTERTON, 1874–1936

A cult is a religion with no political power.

TOM WOLFE, 1931

I prayed for freedom twenty years, but received no answer until I prayed with my legs.

FREDERICK DOUGLASS, 1818–1895

Dare to declare who you are. It is not far from the shores of silence to the boundaries of speech. The path is not long, but the way is deep. You must not only walk there, you must be prepared to leap.

HILDEGARD OF BINGEN, 1098–1179

Chapter 7

One Nation under Pressure

MANY AMERICANS REMEMBER A TIME in their lives when every day in every public school, children recited the Pledge of Allegiance, which declared us "one nation, under God." But there are also people who remember saying the pledge without those words.

It wasn't until Flag Day of 1954 that President Dwight Eisenhower signed the bill to add the phrase "under God" to the Pledge of Allegiance, at a time when the nation was increasingly fearful about nuclear annihilation and the Cold War.

Eisenhower tapped into that fear when he said, "Man everywhere is appalled by the prospect of atomic war. In this somber setting, this law and its effects today have profound meaning. In this way we are reaffirming the transcendence of religious faith in America's heritage and future; in this way we shall constantly strengthen those spiritual weapons which forever will be our country's most powerful resource, in peace or in war."

Eisenhower, who was the first president to read his own inaugural prayer, was an outspoken proponent for an increasingly held view in America: religion—whatever religion—was a force for good, when compared with the Godlessness of Communism.

Ironically, Eisenhower himself was not a member of a church when elected president in 1952, but he joined his wife's Presbyterian church weeks after taking office.

This is the era after World War II when church attendance was peaking, we had prayer in schools, and on Sundays, stores across the country were closed on the "Lord's Day"—even grocery stores. It was the law.

That era of progress and hopefulness continued and the rates of church attendance continued to grow. It was good news for everybody. But in the seats of power in this country, for example, in Congress and at the heads of business was this overly representative group, the mainline Protestants, like the Congregationalists, Presbyterians, and Episcopalians.

Not as much represented in that mixture were Catholics and Jews, as well as denominations that were growing with immigrant waves of Lutherans and others. Black church in all its varieties was making its own history. Suddenly there were great awakenings that were cross-cultural, interracial, and creative. Charismatic Evangelicals, Pentecostals, and other

movements were all in the mix, but not at the top of America's power structure. That was reserved for mainline Protes-
tantism, which in its ignorance presumed everyone was like
them, or at least aspired to be. They set the tone for religious
life, unaware that irrelevance was around the next corner.

From highpoint to decline

One example is a denomination now called the United
Church of Christ, which is made up of several streams,
including the Congregational Church of the Pilgrims who
sailed here on the *Mayflower*. Today the U.C.C is one of the
smallest Christian denominations in the country along
with other churches that define themselves as mainline
Protestant. But its motto in 1957 was "That they may all be
one." Looking back, it was an arrogant statement as that
denomination and others set themselves up at a corporate
headquarters on Riverside Drive in New York City, and
waited for the rest of American Christianity to get there. It
never happened. The percentage of mainline Protestants in
the United States has radically shrunk since the 1960s, and
most of those denominations have moved their headquarters back to the midwestern heartland, too little too late
to stem the tide of their own decline. There were different
theories as to why that decline was so steep and so rapid.

One theory is that during the Vietnam War the mainline Protestant churches got too liberal and alienated all

their members. Then later you see the rise of the more conservative churches. At the time, many presumed these were linked. It was a perceived reason and a perceived tension in the time.

Other theories cite the growing evangelical church. The rise of the religious right was connected to politics but also to megachurches. One theory was that the megachurches are attracting all these former mainline Protestants. That actually also turns out not to be statistically true.

Megachurches did a great job of figuring out how to reach people who wouldn't otherwise be reached in ways that felt comfortable. But to be honest, they attracted a lot of each other's members. Theorists recently have looked at Evangelical Christian birthrates and noted that mainline Protestants just were not having as many kids, and this may be the most overlooked reason for both church decline and church growth.

Christendom is over, thank God

But there was also something else obvious and fundamental going on, a positive tilt toward freedom and away from presumption. Since the 1950s there has been an ever-increasing freedom to choose one's religious home. Some would say that the long-term effects of that have been disastrous and that's why there are so many Nones in America today. Others would say that freedom was long overdue and that it has ushered in an age of more authenticity in religious pursuit—people are in religious community out of choice rather than coercion. I would say that the opportunity within that freedom is for people to really choose a reasonable, rigorous, real faith.

There's a term for those times when Christianity gets wrapped up in empires and nation states: Christendom. Since the first Roman Emperor Constantine converted to Christianity and brought the whole Roman Empire with him, we've had Christendom, a meshing of church and state that was carried forth in centuries to follow.

Even in the USA, the Puritans who had been oppressed by the Anglican Church set sail on the *Mayflower* and set up their own theocracy. There were many other waves after that, some made up of immigrants. You had German Lutherans and German Catholics, and towns with two Catholic churches a block away from each other, one for the Irish and one for the Italians. But with the threat of communism, the Cold War pulled everyone together into one God-fearing anticommunist bunch. Church attendance surged.

Eisenhower's lukewarm endorsement set the stage

In a famous statement, President Eisenhower put it simply: "Our form of government makes no sense unless it is founded in a deeply felt religious belief, and I don't care what it is." In other words, it didn't matter where we worshipped, as long as we went somewhere.

But it wasn't true. There was an implicit assumption that the "somewhere" was somewhere on a Sunday morning. Stores weren't closed for the Jewish Sabbath or for the convenience of Seventh-Day Adventists and other minority religious groups. Stores were closed for the Christian people, whose faith was now wrapped up in the flag, the last stronghold against a people's revolution from the Soviet Bloc.

When many churches look back, they can see their building campaigns and children's programs leading up to that apex, the height, the good old days. That was our American version of Christendom, in the 1950s and '60s, and it is long gone.

Those days are over, and I'm glad. I'm all in favor of religious community and worship attendance, but not at the behest of a fear-based political system. And there was tremendous Christian entitlement there as well. In Christendom, the kingdom and powers in America supported the Christian religion in a manner that felt benign to those who were already a part of it, but today it looks like noblesse oblige and religious privilege. Stores—even gas stations!— closed on Sundays and sports practices didn't interfere with church. That was Christendom, and it made everyone's Christianity a lot easier. Nobody worried about whether the schedule worked for the Jews and those of other faiths.

I don't miss Christendom, I just missed it

My generation never experienced the high church member-ship of Christendom, when you went to your family's church and nothing needed explaining because middle-of-the-road Christianity was the norm. I didn't participate in those "good old days," and I certainly wasn't a pastor during them. In fact, in those good old days as a woman I probably could not have been a large church pastor. The church had to fall into serious decline before outsiders like me got a shot at leadership, in an institution that was already in crisis. I was raised, strayed, became, and stayed a Christian in an age when there was no expectation for me to go to church, and a greater expectation that I would not continue to attend one.

Against generational odds, I stayed in church and even became a pastor. So although I sometimes get whiny and wish more people could experience worship and religious community, I know the answer is not for government to step in and make Christianity easier. Other concerns trump that, like religious freedom.

Besides, in an age of religious choice, I love the idea that, when I am in church somewhere, I am with other people who actually want to be there. They get to choose to be in church. They are not there for business deals, family obli-gation, or public show. The end of Christendom meant the opening up of the religious marketplace. There was sud-denly less obvious pressure and less subtle coercion to attend

Sunday service. But the end of Christendom also heralded changes no one could have anticipated, that most churches were unprepared for. Least prepared of all were the socially entitled congregations like the one Eisenhower joined after becoming president. They were used to the president backing their play. It had been a long time since they had to make a case for what they did or why they existed.

The Rise of the Christian Right

By the mid-1970s, the new culture of Woodstock, hippies, sex, drugs, and rock and roll were in full swing. "Love the One You're With" was not only a hit song but also a mantra for free love and flower power. Jackie Kennedy's pillbox hats and smart suits were no longer fashion icons; they'd been replaced by peasant blouses and Frye boots. Vietnam, Watergate, and Nixon's resignation attested to the chaos this country was experiencing.

Televangelist Pat Robertson, in 1977, created the Christian Broadcasting Network. Its flagship show, *The 700 Club*, almost immediately became one of the most popular shows on cable television. The network was so successful that it became too profitable to remain a nonprofit organization, and in 2001, it was sold to the Walt Disney Company.

Jerry Falwell, a Baptist minister, decided that the separation of religion and politics was the cause of the moral decay in American culture. By founding a group called the

Moral Majority, Falwell was key in establishing the "New Christian Right," a voting bloc to be reckoned with at a national level. The Moral Majority mobilized conservative Americans, mostly churchgoing conservative or Evangelical Christians, to wield the political power that accompanied their sheer numbers. While the Moral Majority no longer officially exists—it was dissolved in 1989—one might argue that its banner has been taken up by what is known today as "the evangelical vote."

So who is an Evangelical?

Over the last few decades, the word itself—"evangelical"—has come to mean many different things to many different people. So much so that the word has come to have a political meaning as well as theological. The Greek root of the word means "good news," which could be seen by some as a tad ironic.

So what is an Evangelical? A 2015 report by the National Association of Evangelicals identified four key statements that define evangelical beliefs, creating what may be the first ever research-driven creed.

Those statements are:

- The Bible is the highest authority for what I believe.

- It is very important for me personally to encourage non-Christians to trust Jesus Christ as their Savior.

- Jesus Christ's death on the cross is the only sacrifice that could remove the penalty of my sin.

- Only those who trust in Jesus Christ alone as their Savior receive God's free gift of eternal salvation.

But just to make things more complicated, the telephone survey also revealed that 41 percent of self-identified Evangelicals fall outside this new definition of evangelical belief, and 21 percent of those who do not call themselves evangelical actually have beliefs that fall within the evangelical definition. It also notes that 23 percent of Catholics and 47 percent of Protestants hold evangelical beliefs.

- 46 percent of Americans who attend church at least weekly hold evangelical beliefs.

- 39 percent of those who identify themselves as Christians hold evangelical beliefs.

- Americans with a high school education or less are most likely to hold evangelical beliefs. Forty percent of those with no more than a high school education strongly agree with all four statements, compared with 26 percent of those with some college, 22 percent of those with bachelor's degrees, and 18 percent of those with graduate degrees.

Post-Christendom Christianity

The history of Christendom and the Moral Majority galls me. None of that represents the Christian Church I call home. I think the end of Christendom was good for the church, in that it gave us a focus we had lost. The Moral Majority hurt the ability of thoughtful Christians to talk about their faith and led many to step away from it. Talk about something to apologize for!

Many Christians, and many who have left the church, are still tired of political candidates and voters who identify as Christian but espouse behaviors that would make Jesus throw them out of the Temple.

How many Christians got tired of repeating, "I'm not like those Christians," and finally stopped talking about the fact that they went to church? The statistics show the decline.

But that must have been particularly hard for the ones who had lived through the high point of church attendance back when Eisenhower reflected a different, more generic, and generous Christianity. Why can't we all just get along? Why can't we go back to Christendom when Christians were calmer and it didn't matter where you worshipped or what doctrine you believed, as long as you were part of a Christian community?

This was the type of low-key Christian that the Democratic candidate Howard Dean seemed to be in 2004. His awkward attempts to talk to Christian Evangelicals in the

South were decried when he exposed his personal ignorance of the Bible by naming Job as his favorite New Testament book. He later corrected himself, noting that Job is actually in the Old Testament.

"I'm a New Englander, so I'm not used to wearing religion on my sleeve and being as open about it," he said in words that many Christians could relate to, including relating to not knowing or caring much about scripture citations themselves. But Howard Dean was pilloried by the Bible-thumping Christians and kicked out of the club that many of us looking in from the outside didn't want to be in ourselves. He was not going to be Christianity's spokesperson or the Democratic Party's savior. The public critique of his laissez-faire Christianity may have led to that, while those who related to his reticence kept quiet or said sorry for a church they were not a member of.

Increasingly, these Christians felt the need to apologize, not for themselves but for the extremist leaders claiming to be moral, claiming to be a majority, whether that was true or not. And many of them just stopped attending church, the first wave of No Ways and No Longers. Apparently, they didn't much miss it. Because if the high point of your worship life was having President Eisenhower congratulate you on your lack of zeal and your regular routine attendance, how much would anyone miss that? I doubt I would.

For me as a post-Christendom Christian, my faith has been a choice (with a few notable exceptions when I was a child or teenager, but let's leave parental bribery and coer cion out of the story for now). Once I was launched, I didn't have to care about religious community but I did. Yet with that caring came the growing need to apologize.

Politicians and the perception problem

The 2016 presidential race provided a spectacle—actually many spectacles—of Christianity's staggering perception problem. Early on, Dr. Ben Carson asserted that he "would not advocate that we put a Muslim in charge of this nation" when asked if he thought a Muslim should be allowed to run for president. During the height of the primaries, *Christianity Today*, a prominent evangelical magazine, ran articles titled "The Theology of Ted Cruz" and "The Theology of Donald Trump" that included the following:

Ted Cruz's "campaign is perhaps best described as a reclamation project. He wants to 'restore'...or 'reclaim' the 'Judeo-Christian values' that he believes are 'the foundation of this nation'". The article goes on to point out that Cruz believes that the United States was founded as a Christian nation based on Judeo-Christian principles. This got challenged more than once. The group of evangelical African-American pastors who met at Wheaton College in October 2013 to denounce the "let's return America to its Christian roots" rhetoric that the Cruz campaign espoused argued that the United States was built on the backs of slaves rather than Judeo-Christian principles.

"A master at fusing evangelical Christianity and presidential politics," the writer goes on to say, "he tells the men and women at Community Bible Church that 'weeping may endure for a night, but joy comes in the morning' (Psalm 30:5)." Today one is left to wonder whether Cruz was referring to inauguration morning.

Donald Trump's theology has been explored in multiple media outlets, including the *Christianity Today* article, which questioned his evangelical theology. He had been described as the candidate most likely to be identified as evangelical, whether it is true or not. The magazine pointed out the conflict between Trump's positions including his support of the use of torture, his apparent lack of sin (he announced that he has never asked God for forgiveness because he doesn't really do anything that would require it), and the importance of winning at all costs (because he "hates losers"). The Bible is Trump's favorite book (like a good movie, "it gets better every time you look at it"). This is saying a lot, because he likes it even better than his "all-time second-favorite book, *The Art of the Deal.*"

In March 2016, *The Washington Post* reported that, "One of the most surprising parts of the 2016 election has been evangelical Christian support for Donald Trump." In the twenty states where primary or caucus exit polls had been conducted, Trump had won an average of 36 percent of the "white born-again evangelical Christian" vote. The article went on to point out that the Evangelicals have their own None problem, and that "Trump does best among

Evangelicals with one key trait: They don't really go to church," thus making the point that not all self-described Evangelicals are the same. Apparently there are "less devout" and "more devout" Evangelicals, and the less devout like Trump more than the more devout.

Ant that's just the tip of the iceberg.

and

Politicians and perception

Presidential races impact Americans' perceptions of Christians, usually for the worse. Is it because politicians are poor examples? I don't think they are any worse than most people, but their bad behavior in the name of God gets a lot more press.

If people are turned off by exclusive salvation views and anti-Islamic rhetoric, they're going to be even more turned off by some of our political candidates. But while much attention is given to what the candidates say about their own faith, and whether or not it is right, wrong, or unfaithful, I am most disturbed by what the candidates say about each other's faith.

For example, when Christian candidates accuse one another of not being Christian, they conform to the worse stereotypes of judgmental Christians, who eat their own and cannibalize each other. "Look at these Christians, how they love one another," mused the early historian Tertullian (ca. 160–220), imagining that pagans would be impressed and converted by our care for one another. I don't think you see much of that caring in the political campaigns or their coverage.

But in reality, churches are full of people from different political parties who do care for one another. They may disagree on everything political, but they still bring casseroles to the grieving and arrange the flowers at one another's funerals.

They teach one another's kids at Vacation Bible School, and when little Johnny pounds little Freddie on the head with a nearby Bible, and little Freddie responds by throwing juice on little Johnny, and little Freddie retaliates by smearing glue and glitter on little Johnny's picture of the baby Jesus, no adult, Democrat or Republican, gets to tell these six-year-olds that they do not deserve to be called Christians.

Little Johnny and little Freddie are not consistently practicing love, kindness, forgiveness, or grace, but they are still loved by their teachers and held by a body, the church, that has come to understand that this is what it means to be human. Adults have the same selfish and violent impulses as children. We don't send our children to spend a week at Vacation Bible School because they already have this all figured out. We admit they need help and training. And we don't show up at church as adults as a way of announcing our own righteousness. We come because we still need to hear a word from the Prince of Peace and the God of love.

So the continual criticizing of one another from a distance and in public is distasteful, especially to people who don't go to church. They've never experienced the breakup of a six-year-old fight on the church playground, and the joy that teacher has when those kids grow up to be a little kinder to each other the next summer.

Instead they think, Christianity is about being good all the time and getting it right. And when you don't, your fellow Christians call you un-Christian and they kick you out. Who wants to be a part of that?

A ban on Muslims is a ban on us all

Christians don't like it when they get accused of being responsible for all the world's warfare. If they are even aware of the stereotype, that is. Many seem to be oblivious to how they are perceived by the Nones. Otherwise, why would they accuse other religions of the same thing?

A ban on Muslims and a wall at the border of Mexico are hard to square with loving your neighbor as yourself. Islam is not responsible for all the world's warfare any more than Christianity is. A ban on Muslims is a ban on us all.

Speaking of how people die, more people die by being murdered than die in warfare. In the case of murder, the higher the percentage of Muslims in a society, the lower the homicide rate, said a 2011 study by University of California, Berkeley.

An openly SBNR candidate is good for us

Bernie Sanders, the first Jewish presidential candidate, may also be the first serious SBNR candidate. Though raised Jewish, Sanders says that he is "not particularly religious," nor is he a member of any congregation or synagogue. "I am not actively involved in organized religion," he has told reporters. In *Outsider in the White House*, his autobiography, he makes no mention of the months he spent on a kibbutz in northern Israel. As a Jewish-American politician, his experience on the kibbutz did more to bolster his faith in socialism than in God or Judaism.

However, he has not come out as an atheist and is careful not to come off as antireligious. He has toured black churches, spoken to Evangelicals at Liberty University in Virginia, and addressed the Pontifical Academy of Social Sciences at the Vatican.

When asked by ABC's Jimmy Kimmel if he believed in God, Sanders reflected his knowledge of the Torah by saying, "Well, you know, I am who I am," words from God to Moses via the burning bush.

"And what I believe in, what my spirituality is about, is that we're all in this together—that I think it's not a good thing to believe, as human beings, that we can turn our backs on the suffering of other people.

"And this is not Judaism," Sanders continued, sounding like a No Longer, or someone in the SBNR camp, pulling from other religious traditions while referencing a vague sense of personal spirituality. "This is what Pope Francis is talking about: That we cannot worship just billionaires and the making of more and more money. Life is more than that."

A 2015 Pew survey revealed that Americans don't really know what religion Sanders is. Nearly a third say Sanders is "somewhat" religious; nearly a third say he's not, and more than a quarter say they don't know. But one thing is clear: His supporters do not hold that against him, and he is the first major candidate to resist the old categories, which places him in a number of new categories. Like most American Jews, the senator from Vermont is perceived according to a Pew survey conducted in 2013, as proud to be Jewish, but not connected to a synagogue or temple.

Sanders appeals to more than SBNRs. He also appeals to people of faith who participate in religious community. His respect for many traditions plays well, especially to those who wish all religious people could be similarly open-minded. Like many Nones, Sanders is still inspired by Pope Francis and the Dalai Lama, but unwilling to sign up for the traditions they espouse. It's no surprise to hear this from a candidate who resonates so well with young people.

He reminds me of the many people I went to college with, who were against organized religion but would read a book or two and then declare, "I consider myself to be a Buddhist."

To which I always wanted to respond, "Does any Buddhist consider you to be a Buddhist?"

As for burning in hell, Sanders shares the right-here-right-now concerns of his supporter Ron Reagan for the hell on earth that we call injustice. But Sanders is kinder toward the religious, making room for them in the "not worried about burning in hell" camp, so much so that atheists wish he were a little more on their side.

I'm glad Bernie Sanders can say what he wants to and refuse to say more than that about the religious life he chooses not to live. I'm glad the atheist Ron Reagan doesn't worry about burning in hell. I'm glad that religious community is optional and therefore freely chosen. In the large space between "whatever floats your boat" and "burn in hell," freely chosen religious communities are varied, rich, and changing, but still way too much of a secret. I wish more people knew how good religious community can be when it is reasonable, rigorous, and real.

Chapter 8

Please Read Responsibly

O NE OF THE HARDEST AND most rewarding aspects of faith is the rigorous reading of a sacred text. I struggle with what the Bible says in certain places, but as a library, a collection of books, it has become a lens through which I see the world and remember that I am not the first generation to experience whatever I think is uniquely troubling to me.

You can tell when someone deals earnestly with a sacred text, and my first clue is that they do not spend a bunch of time quoting the five lines they have memorized about their favorite hot button issue. Anyone who actually deals with the Bible knows that "proof-texting" is an unfair way to use that rich resource.

They have a better sense of what the text says and what it doesn't say. Which is why Donald Trump got caught out in 2015 when he quoted the Bible with something no one can find there. "There's so many things that you can learn from it [The Bible]. Proverbs, the chapter 'never bend to envy,'" he said. "I've had that thing all of my life where people are bending to envy. Actually it's an incredible book, so many things you can learn from the Bible and you can lead your life. I'm not just talking in terms of religion; I'm talking in terms of leading a life even beyond religion. There are so many brilliant things in the Bible."

After spotting a supporter carrying a copy of *The Art of the Deal*, Trump told the crowd that his own best-seller was his second favorite book, after the Bible. "Nothing beats the Bible. Nothing beats the Bible. Not *The Art of the Deal*. Not even close."

What a compliment. It's the type of praise that comes with utter unfamiliarity. If Trump spent some time with the Bible, he'd probably like his own book more and the Bible less.

Let's be straightforward here with clear eyes. The Bible is a hard book to love. Anyone who denies that has probably not read much of it.

Pious Amnesia

An ancient and powerful ruler felt bad that his country had not been very faithful, so in a sudden moment of religious remorse, he declared a massive religious celebration and demanded everyone's attendance. Apparently, everyone felt pretty great afterward. Despite being forced to show up, the people actually experienced something divine and mysterious in the celebration.

And feeling suddenly close to God and to one another, they did what comes naturally in such situations. They agreed that anyone who did not feel equally passionate about God should be killed.

This couldn't be in the Bible. It must be a fable. Actually, you can find the story of King Asa in 2 Chronicles 15:1–15, but trust me, I've given you the highlights. This is not the kind of Bible story people keep by their bedsides for daily inspiration. But it is in the Bible so let's get back to it.

In a fit of self-righteousness, the same people who had drifted from God had the nerve to put out a death sentence on anyone else that had drifted from God.

And by the way, how would they judge such a thing? Did they take attendance at the big religious spectacle from the day before and kill anyone who was truant? I'm all for regular worship attendance, but this seems a bit extreme. King Asa's forced celebration and the impulse to kill anyone who missed it are not unique in scripture. This is not the first time that religious fervor got disconnected from its true base, which is love. It won't be the last time either. I think stories like this are in the Bible to remind us what jerks we can be when we think we are being religious. Worked up and courageous in a crowd, they pointed their fingers at others, but really, they were pointing their fingers at themselves.

Sometimes, a genuine experience of God becomes a pious amnesia. The newly inspired forget what they were like before.

Nobody wants an invitation with a death sentence attached. I don't have to apologize for the existence of such stories, either in scripture or in history. But I do have to read them in order to remind myself that I'm capable of pious amnesia, too.

Yes, sometimes history is written by the winners. When that happens in the Bible, such winners have been known to add theologically suspect postscripts to otherwise excellent stories. They'll imply that God killed one branch of the human family in order that another branch could live and do an absolutely super job ruling everybody for a few generations. All that this shows is that the manipulation of history in the name of politics, power, and religion is so old that you can find it in the Bible, too.

We're not the first generation of geniuses

There's another tradition, thousands of years old, where rabbis, theologians, preachers, and reformers actually debate, argue, and interpret these things in scripture. Rabbis wrote down their dissenting opinions in the Midrash, and Christians have debated each other in sermons, prophecies, or angry letters nailed to a cathedral door. We have a long-documented history of dissent, debate, and deep listening for the divine truth in scripture.

It's not a once-and-for-all decision, but a conversation we get to be a part of, because God is still speaking.

Are we the first generation of geniuses to notice that there are common myths among religious traditions? No, but we may be the generation most likely to give ourselves a gold star for noticing it, as if we are cleverer than the past generations who put the Bible together full of internal contradictions as well as stories that do not appear to be entirely original. We may be the generation most likely to then label all such stories "untrue." Why don't we, instead, say to ourselves, "Factual or not, there may be a larger truth here that might be of value. Maybe I should read this for content rather than treating it like the true-or-false section of a standardized test."

And here's another thought: Perhaps our beliefs do not ultimately determine whether or not something is true. Perhaps it doesn't matter whether or not I believe in aliens; either they exist or they don't—no matter what you or I believe. Truth isn't required to be "reasonable" or "believable"—it's just required to be true.

Who taught you kids this stuff?

At a pretty free-thinking church, where we taught our kids to question and read the Bible intellectually as both God-inspired and as literature, I was surprised when I saw my first batch of eighth-grade confirmation papers. These were the papers that the young people wrote after years of children's Sunday school and other training in the fundamentals of the Christian faith.

After years of preparation, they had learned and become

mature enough to decide for themselves whether or not they wanted to join the church as adult members.

So I was surprised to read in many of their papers ambivalence based on concern that the church embraced a strong fundamentalist strain of theology. They were pushing back against it, but they seemed to be pushing back as though all of us in their church believed it.

Some wrote, "I'm just not sure I should get confirmed and join the church as an adult member...I'm just not sure I should take that step, because I don't believe the world was created in six days."

I asked them, "Who in this church told you they believe the world was created in six days? Or that you had to believe it?" I was hopping mad. I wanted those renegade volunteers' names so that they could receive the appropriate theological beat down, or at least a few polite questions. When I pressed those kids, they acknowledged that they didn't hear that stuff in Sunday school class and they had not heard it from their parents.

Some said they didn't want to join the church because they didn't believe gay people were condemned. But nobody in their church was telling them to interpret one line of scripture about homosexuality literally and ignore the rest of the page about shellfish. It was because that's what the outside world told them that Christians believed.

Somewhere in the culture they were getting the idea that real Christians believe that you have to take scripture literally, the way fundamentalist Christians do. So being eighth graders, and therefore experts on what is wrong with everything, they did what came naturally. They took an idea like the world was literally created in six days and they looked for the hole in the argument.

That's not too hard to do, but being eighth graders, they assumed their insights were unique, daring, and definitive. "They don't even mention the dinosaurs in the Bible but we know that dinosaurs existed. Therefore, the Bible can't be true because they missed something huge: dinosaurs missing...hello??"

Their conclusion was that if you could find a flaw in the Bible then that meant you were not a Christian. You believed instead in this scientific theory of evolution. I wanted to say, "Who in this church told you to think science and evolution were at odds with your faith? Who here told you we were creationists?"

But they didn't hear it from us. They hear it on the news where the weirdest voices of Christianity get way too much airtime. If there's a tsunami, an earthquake, a heat wave, or a drought, chances are some professional Christian will say that it's God's way of getting our attention and therefore it must be someone's fault.

After Orlando

When Disney World introduced "Gay Days," Pat Robertson ominously reminded the people of Orlando that they were in a hurricane zone, and speculated, "It'll bring about terrorist bombs; it'll bring earthquakes, tornadoes, and possibly a meteor." After the 2016 massacre of 49 people in a gay club in Orlando, I am more committed than ever to telling a different Christian story. I can't control what people like Robertson say, but I can point out how that news coverage affects thoughtful people of faith. In the past it has silenced us, but we can't allow that silence to continue. It's time for real conversations among real people. Whether we end up on the news or not, we have to at least speak to each other. "Where two or three are gathered, there I am with you," Jesus promised, as if to encourage us to keep thinking and talking.

Hearing from those eighth graders at my church taught me something. No matter how much you teach within the circle of your own religious community, there are these dominant ideas about religion that are out in the culture, coming from other people, and they play a huge role in how we talk about the church. This has never been truer than during the 2016 presidential campaigns, where Tea Party–esque, gun-toting, Muslim-bashing people who believe they have a corner on the Christian faith—form the base that may determine who becomes President of the United States. And it was agonizing to hear that loudmouthed voice after the Orlando shooting.

If there were ever a time when Americans who call themselves Christians yet do not share those beliefs should speak up—at least to their children—it is now. Make it clear that there are other Christians who don't spread hate and fear, because we don't believe that Jesus spread hate and fear either.

Those eighth graders in my confirmation class were paradigmatic of the adults, just more honest about their questions. After all, no one asks our adult members to write papers before joining the church. I suspect some of them would have said the same thing the kids did that they worried they were frauds for thinking that science made sense.

This obsession with belief is fascinating, because the Fundamentalists who claim that they're following scripture ignore what Jesus says and does. For Jesus, in general, faith and belief were what you do and how you act. For instance, when he says, "Do you believe?" it generally means, "Do you step forward? Are you willing to follow me? Are you willing to try this?" He seldom says, "Do you believe?" He doesn't ask for anyone to give a long theological discourse. There's no moment when Jesus recites the Nicene Creed about himself. He says many things about himself, but they're highly mystical: "I am the way, the truth, the light." What does that mean? He leaves it there, complicated. He never says, "I demand that you believe my mother was a virgin." Jesus never asks anybody to sign a statement of faith. So why would we?

When the fundamentalist movement commandeered the word "Christian," faith came to be associated with intellectual certainty. So you have one group of Christians who says, "This is what you have to believe"; but then you have another who says, "Well, I can't believe in that with intellectual certainty," or "I believe that sometimes, and other times I don't." Either way that second silenced group wonders: Is there room for me in this church? Or should I just opt out?

Chapter 9

This Certainty Is Killing Me

WE DON'T HAVE A PROBLEM of doubt; we have a problem of certainty. That actually reflects American culture in general. Consider the world of politics. There is no room for nuance. There is no room for changing your mind. If the Constitution says that everyone has the right to bear arms, then everyone should have a gun if they want one. This despite the fact that in the centuries since the Constitution was written and amended, shopping malls, airplanes, and AK-57s have been invented. And at the time the Constitution was written, the writers were creating a nation where arms were needed to take land from indigenous people, extract unpaid labor from enslaved people, and break from paying taxes on what that land and labor generated. But there's no room for questions. We are stuck in our certainty.

There's very little in the Bible to support human certainty about much of anything, beginning with our first story in the book of Genesis. God did not have to put the tree of good and evil in the Garden of Eden and tempt Adam and Eve. The Almighty—who was in charge of everything—could have left that temptation out.

But the Creator decided to give humans a choice, and they chose to eat the forbidden fruit. We can go around saying it was the Serpent's fault. Then Adam blames Eve. The truth is they did what they were thinking about. They made a choice.

We are told that eating the fruit gave them the knowledge of good and evil. That makes sense. You don't understand the difference between good and evil until you have dipped into both. So they disobey the command to avoid the tree, they eat the fruit, and the narrative goes that they are suddenly ashamed and hence they are kicked out of the Garden of Eden. Were they kicked out? Or were they freed?

God could have created us like pampered little house cats, where God would deliver a little bowl of water and a little bit of food and we'd be confined to this Garden of Eden and we couldn't get out and we'd be brushed and taken care of and loved. Instead, God puts this little cat flap door on the edge and says, "I dare you to step through that cat flap, Mittens."

Adam and Eve take the dare. I've always believed they were freed for adventure more than kicked out of paradise.

They were freed to use their brains, to explore the natural world and how it was made.

The Garden of Eden was not an intellectual desert

So how did we go from that story with all its depth and nuance to creationism? When did we stop seeing that story as a deep description of the human desire for choice and growth? When did we start using the book of Genesis as a dim-witted timetable for how the world was created?

How did we get here? How did American Christianity end up in an intellectual desert of bad history and childlike rigidity? And why don't Christians talk more about it? For most of the history of religious communities around the world, science has been the friend of religion. If "religion" means community and together we serve and worship God, scientific discoveries should convince us that God is even more amazing than we knew before. And many scientists will tell you exactly that, that their work enhances their faith in a divine Creator.

So what happened to Christianity's public relations department that we got saddled with the reputation of hating science, or disbelieving obvious things? Well, you can tell me about Galileo and Copernicus and other scientists being persecuted by the church. You can tell me about the Scopes monkey trial in which Americans got publicly fascinated with this so-called conflict between the creationists and the evolutionists.

But for every one story like that, there are a thousand years of working together, and of religious people encouraging education, study, research in all fields including science and medicine. So when did Fundamentalists win the PR battle that leaves eighth graders worried that by joining church they are putting on a dunce's cap?

Don't blame Darwin

To understand this issue today, it always helps to go back to history, and here, while I could take you all the way back to the dinosaurs and the eight-track tapes they used to listen to, I won't. Instead let's go back to where many of us first learn about this conflict beginning, to the tension that was created in 1859 when Charles Darwin published *On the Origin of Species*. That was a work of scientific literature many of us are familiar with that put forth this idea of evolutionary biology.

Darwin pointed out and demonstrated something that was relatively observable and reasonable, that there are mutations that occur in species and you can track them with fossils and other evidences, and that given certain environmental conditions, those mutations will either help the species to continue or hurt them. Through this process of natural selection, they will continue or they will not.

Biology books can give you thousands of examples of how this works.

In terms of religious history, at least within this country, an alternative point of view arose called creationism. Proponents were people who were presumed to take the creation story as the model, instead of evolution, there beginning this false dichotomy that people of faith have to choose between one or the other.

You either believe this scientific theory that, when presented, particularly in an elementary way when you're in grade school, sounds pretty reasonable, or you accept that all that stuff that sounds reasonable is not true and that all this really happened in six days, and if you don't believe it, you're not a Christian.

If I were Satan and I wanted to destroy every good thing in Christianity, that's the dichotomy I'd set up. It would ensure that all the smart people stayed away and all the idiots stayed in. History would take care of the rest. Guess how? Through a process of natural selection. Nobody would join this group. That's what I would do if I wanted to destroy every good thing in the church.

Actually, as in so many cases, Satan doesn't even have to do that, because we do it to ourselves. In this case, it was the fundamentalist movement around 1929. Darwin's work came out in 1859, but in 1929, the term "creationism" first starts to be associated with Christian Fundamentalists making statements about the literal interpretation of Genesis.

Rejecting the reasonable

They were reacting to some cutting-edge Bible scholarship coming over from Germany that was pointing out what is now considered obvious: that there are different and contradictory narratives in scripture. If you read scripture, you understand that certain things were written down at one time, and certain things were written down at another, and they might end up under the same title. This reasonable Bible scholarship was coming over to the United States from Germany.

The American Christians who would become the fundamentalist movement experienced that scholarship as threatening to blow apart all they held dear. What they missed was that the internal tensions in scripture were there from the beginning, even in the creation story. The Germans didn't invent the contradiction. It was built into the library that got put together and called "the Bible."

I think we were always meant to notice the discrepancies and learn from them. For example take the line in Genesis that reads, "God spoke, 'Let us make human beings in our image.'" Did you ever hear that? "Our image"? That's accurate as a translation. But this is a part of Genesis that the creationists won't touch with a ten-foot pole.

"Make them reflecting our nature so they can be responsible for the fish in the sea, the birds in the air, the cattle, and, yes, earth itself. God created human beings. He created them male and female." In our image. Right there in the first chapter of Genesis is this idea that if we are created in God's image, male and female, God is male and female.

You may remember something about a rib. Adam is all by himself, and he's lonely, and God says, "Well, I'll create Eve out of your rib, and she's going to be your helpmate. Then I'm going to give you guys dominion over everything, but you can have dominion over Eve, and she's going to have pain in childbirth." Where's that in this? Well, it's in the Bible; it just comes later.

In fact, it resides right next to this radically different understanding of God wanting to create male and female human beings in "our" image.

You have one story over here about a rib, where Eve is created to do whatever Adam doesn't want to do around the house, including have babies presumably, and she's going to feel pain for it.

And then over there you have this beautiful philosophical story. "Create them in our image," God says. Our image, male and female. These very different ideas share shelf space together in the library of books we call the Bible.

Creationism and contradictions

In 1929, when the word "creationism" came to be associated with fundamentalism in this country, it's not like nobody had ever noticed the contradictions before. Back in the second century, the early Christians deliberately put the Bible together with all these contradictions right there in it.

But the fundamentalist movement was about denying the contradictions and instead making a list of what they thought Christianity had to be. What are the essentials? What are the "fundamentals" of the faith? The nonnegotiables? One they came up with was creationism: rigid ideas about the world being created literally in six days.

It's actually in Darwin's private correspondence that he started referring to these people as "creationists." They don't originally think that's what they are. They think they're holding the line about ideas coming over from the continent that threaten their worldview. They are trying to fit literal understanding into a story that was never created as a historical document or a scientific treatise but as poetry to imply God's hand was involved in everything.

It makes the rather edifying point that we human beings were created last. God spent five days on everything else, and we got just that one day. We are not all that and a bag of chips. You could say we were creation's culmination, or you could say we were an afterthought, slopped together at the tail end of a long workweek. The major point is this: It is not, and was not, all about us.

That's the healthy debate that has always been a part of Judaism, through Midrash, and conversation in church. Many Christians for centuries have talked about the easy way in which science and religion can walk together.

Still, because of the relatively recent blip of fundamentalism, in the public eye, there is a perception they cannot. In response to that, Galileo gets more press in history than centuries of church-sponsored science. So much so that an eighth grader in my church might write in his paper, "I don't think the world was created in six days, so I'm not sure I'm a Christian."

Later, creationism gives itself a makeover and a new name, "Intelligent Design," which maintains that nature is too complex to be explained solely by the theory of evolution and that there actually is some unspecified intelligent source that has designed the universe. That sounds good to me. When I first heard the term "Intelligent Design," I liked it. But once you learn what is meant by it, you discover it is nothing more than warmed-over creationism, over and against evolution.

When you dig underneath the term "intelligent design," at least in the culture wars of this country, you find a serious hostility toward the science of evolution, the church at its antiscientific worst.

They want the Intelligent Design worldview to be taught in public schools alongside the scientific theory of evolution, because they are opposed to the theory of evolution. They are still trying to work the science into a literal interpretation of the creation myth, like stuffing a ten-pound sausage into a five-pound bag.

Yet we dig in on all sides. We are all so quick to take offense. In our society, that's our way. "I'm offended. Game over. We're not talking anymore." On the evolution side, there are people who will say, "I'm outraged that you would even call it a theory of evolution. It's fact, not theory. That's insulting," as though theories in science don't mean something.

In the scientific world, it's not an insult to call something a theory. A theory is something that is well researched, that you take seriously. In the scientific world, there's a huge difference between confirmed theories and wild conjectures. So the polemic on that side is, "Don't call it a theory." But it is a theory. In science, everything is a theory.

The tension here might be that evolution is a theory, not an explanation. Science really can't give us explanations. It can give us theories and explain patterns to us, and that's really helpful. It can show us that certain patterns produce certain results, but those patterns are not always psychologically satisfying and often don't ask or answer the deeper question that religion asks and seeks to answer: "But why?"

Fear and the frontal lobe

I recently learned that the frontal lobe of the human brain does not get finished and closed until the age of twenty-five. Until you're twenty-five, your brain is still under construction and you're prone to rash decisions, impulses, emotions. This was devastating news for me as a parent. I have really been looking forward to the day I can stop worrying so much. Turns out the date will be years later than I had thought. But of course, when I remember myself at twenty-five, the theory about the frontal lobe being undeveloped makes sense.

So what do you do with that information? If I were designing humanity myself, I would like to have all that stuff nailed down around age one, and then you can choose a career at age two and start supporting your parents.

So what do you make of this scientific theory that your frontal lobe remains under construction until the age of twenty-five? Do you say, "Well, I'm not going to make any decisions until I'm twenty-five"? Good luck with that.

It does cause us to look back and think, "What does it mean when I thought I was being led to do something in my younger days? What was that? Was that real? Was that about other people? Was that God speaking to me? Or was it just that my frontal lobe hadn't closed?" You can blame a lot on that frontal lobe.

But before you get all smug about your decision-making ability if you are on the other side of twenty-five, there's bad news associated with that, too. Apparently, the moment that closes, it's downhill from there in terms of your brain's ability to work. You reach this high point at twenty-five, and then you start deteriorating from then on in terms of concentration and memory. And sad to say, when I look at my own life, that part makes sense, too.

I wish I had known how important that twenty-fifth year was back when I was going through it. I should have invested in stocks or taken my IQ test and had it framed.

Maybe we should teach that theory to people before they are twenty-five so they can make all their big decisions in that one year and write them down and then never be released from them, because it's all falling apart in the decades to follow.

Twenty-five as the apex of intelligence means wisdom is greater than intelligence. Understanding is greater than our brains. There's probably more to creation than simply design or engineering. And those are profoundly religious ideas. They are not at odds with science but they work alongside it.

I'm grateful I have more to rely on than my own closed-up, deteriorating, frontal-lobe-heavy brain. I give thanks for the scientists. I give thanks for the theologians. I give thanks for a loving God who created the universe in ways I'll probably never understand in this life but one day perhaps will understand in heaven and truly say, "How great thou art."

Chapter 10

I'm a Pastor and I Don't Care What You Believe

A MINISTER TOLD ME A story about a family who wanted to have their baby baptized. The mother had grown up in the church. He and the mother and father had a nice meeting to talk about the baptism, but after the meeting, before the Sunday when the baptism was going to take place, the father wrote the minister a lengthy e-mail, saying, "I have to tell you that I don't know if I should stand up there and do this baptism because I'm an atheist. I don't know if I can, in good conscience, say that I'm going to raise my child in the church, when I don't believe this."

The minister and the father met, and the minister described their discussion, saying, "The more we talked,

I realized, this man wasn't really an atheist. He didn't really believe that God did not exist; he was more of an agnostic. He had questions. He had doubts. He wondered about things. When I pressed him on what it was he felt he had to believe in order to go on with the baptism, he listed a litany of doctrines from a very conservative fundamentalist church from his childhood. And because he didn't believe those things, he wasn't sure he could stand up in this church and have his baby baptized. What I told that father was, 'You're welcome to stand up and have your baby baptized. Are you going to come to church? Are you going to bring your child to church?' The father said, 'Yes. Yes. I'm just not sure I believe all that stuff.' "

The pastor said, "You're welcome here. I'm your pastor."

Outside, looking in

It reminds me of a Bible story, where Jesus heals an epileptic boy. You have this father who is standing on the outside of this community looking in. There are these people who are all excited about Jesus, and hopeful that he can heal them, listening to his message and trying to live according to his teachings.

Then you have this other group over there, Pharisees, who are quizzing Jesus about what he believes. They're having this theological and religious argument, while this poor suffering dad is looking in from the outside, saying,

"I really want to bring my kid into this, because we need some help; but I don't know what I believe."

As parents, you are only as happy as your least happy child. That's what this father was going through. He has this son, a wonderful little boy who likes to do all the things little kids like to do. He likes to run, and he likes to go off and have adventures, and he likes to go swimming. But he's got this physical ailment that today we would call seizure disorder, or epilepsy, and the father has to raise his little boy to be both courageous and cautious, balancing encouragement with lifesaving warnings about everything that could go wrong.

"What if you have a seizure and you're playing near the water? What if you fell into the water and you drowned? If you're playing near the fire, what if you have a seizure and you burn yourself? If you're playing and running around near the edge of a cliff, what if you have a seizure and fall to your death?" I imagine the father's constant fear and worry, but not just for his son's physical well-being. He was probably also worried about his son's place in the community. At that time, many people thought that a seizure meant you were possessed by a demon.

So, if your child had seizures, he or she would probably be excluded by the community in virtually every way. People would be suspicious and fearful. They wouldn't let their children play with your little boy. How do you talk to your child about that? He had run out of words.

So, this father had heard about Jesus and hoped that

Jesus might have the power to do something about this, to heal the boy, to heal their lives, to heal the unspeakable hurt of a parent who cannot stem his child's pain. And in the story, the dad is at the edge of this circle, trying to figure out if he can step in.

Martin Luther King Jr. once said, "Faith is taking the first step, even when you cannot see the whole staircase." This is what Jesus ends up saying to the boy's father. "Do you have faith?" I believe it's a way to ask him, "Will you step out, and step forward?" To the father of the epileptic boy, Jesus conveys, "You are welcome here. Will you step into the circle? Do you believe? Don't think about it, just step."

I'm not going to address the question of how the child was healed. To me, that's a mystery. Every illness and every healing is a mystery. What I'm interested in is this dad, this character, and how Jesus treats him. I think this dad is right here. He's us. I relate to this dad.

In the story the dad comes forward, gets his courage up, walks up to the circle, and asks for help with his son, but at first, he's talking to the disciples, not Jesus. The disciples are not able to fix things, so they go to Jesus.

The poor dad, we already know that he is shy. Now, he's got to step forward again, in the spotlight of Jesus' total attention. Everyone who wanted Jesus' attention that day is looking at this dad, and expecting something.

And Jesus tells him that anything is possible, if you believe.

You can just imagine the dad saying, "You're kidding me? It's all about that? But what if I don't believe? Will there be a quiz?"

But the dad doesn't show any of that at first. He has one priority. He has this chance to have his son healed.

"Anything is possible if you believe," he is told when he gets to the front of the line.

Well, what would you say?

"Okay, fine, I'm just going to say it," he thinks, and then says out loud, "I believe."

Maybe he does believe, perhaps a little.

But then he has this internal dialogue where he must think, "Well, I don't know if I believe all of that. Will it hurt the healing that I am not sure? And by the way, believe what? Can someone review the questions with me? What have I just done? Have I just lied at the moment of my son's greatest need?" The poor dad is honest and raw. He can't help himself.

So, in this amazing story, all of a sudden he just tells the truth and adds to his statement, qualifies it to make sure it's true and captures the complexity of all he feels and who he is: "I believe, but help my unbelief."

At first, he says what's expected: "Of course I believe, now heal my son already." He says what he thinks he needs to say to get the job done.

But then, standing in the presence of Jesus, he cannot tell a lie, even if it is needed, even if he wants to believe, even if he believes just a little, or plans to believe after this, if only, if only God will heal his son.

But as his "Yes, I believe" statement hangs out there with more certainty than he actually has, he has to say more. He has to be real. When they really talk to him, Jesus has been known to have that effect on people.

The father has to bring who he is; he has to bring his integrity; he has to admit that he also has unbelief. So he says it. "I believe, but help my unbelief."

And in response, what does Jesus say? He does *not* say, "Well then, sorry about your son, you've blown it; I won't be working with you."

Jesus doesn't care what the father believes

No, Jesus seems fine with the man's words, unfazed by the news that the father is a mix of belief and unbelief. What's so powerful about this story is that the dad admits his unbelief, and Jesus does not care.

Jesus does not care. He ministers to the father and to the son anyway.

I imagine this incredible thing happening in this moment of community—not just to the dad, but to every-body who's watching it. They've all learned something. They've all seen a desperate dad say, under pressure, "I believe, I'll sign on." But then they also see that he can't lie, he's got to tell the truth in the light at that moment. "Help my unbelief, too."

To which Jesus beckons him to come on in, and everybody sees it happen. Jesus talks and asks questions about belief, but clearly, it is not a deal breaker.

That's how I imagine it happened. That father, terrified of joining community, steps in anyway. And when he does, he feels something healing pulling him in and he goes for it.

Like an atheist dad at his son's baptism, like so many people before and after him, he takes the first step of faith. You don't have to see the whole staircase.

Do you believe in the possibility of a community of faith? Then step on in. You don't need to see the whole staircase. You can even say as you enter, "Help my unbelief." Take me just as I am.

Stop agonizing over what you believe, as if that determines whether or not you can be in church. Stop wondering whether atheists would consider you a Christian. Stop worrying about what other Christians think about you. Your beliefs are not that important. You're not that important. I'm not that important.

Heaven has got to be a lot more interesting than a debate about doctrine. If heaven is a place with a theological checklist, I don't want to go.

For centuries, millennia even, religions have existed without knowing whether or not you believe in them. Our belief obsession is something strange and recent. Religion at its best focuses on how to live, not what to think.

So to base religious community on a onetime belief statement? It seems to fly in the face of the creation story and the scientific evidence. Of course your mind will change. That's why you have a mind.

You can be in community or not be in community. But your membership should be freely chosen, not forced or at the whim of your changing intellectual assents about doctrine, science, or theology.

I'm a pastor and I don't care what you believe. I don't think God does either.

Chapter 11

Religion Is Rigorous Because Practice Matters

Freedom to choose religion is good. But the choice is significant and it won't come easy. There are a million other ways to spend your time. And these days it is countercultural to spend any time worshipping something other than yourself. People will think you are crazy. You may be tempted to downplay it, or make other choices instead.

But practice matters. Doing something more than once on a regular basis makes it better. Open-minded people of faith seem to accept that about all areas of life, except their own faith practice, which they tend to downplay. We've talked about why that is (the fear of appearing to impose your views on others, the fear of being mistaken for a fundamentalist, the fear of speaking about our faith), but now let's talk about why it matters. Practice is important, and for religious people, our central practice is worship.

We may feed the hungry, visit the sick, and love our enemies, but nonreligious people can do all those things as well or as poorly as religious people. What sets us apart is our practice: worshipping God in the company of other people in a tradition larger and older than we are. Our practice has been handed down to us for centuries, so why in this century would we want to downplay it? Religion is rigorous, it requires something of us, that is more important than what we believe or confess to believe. Religion requires this weird practice of worship, which is not about hiding from the world but transforming it. Through worship we hope to be better than we would have been otherwise, and for that to work, we need to show up.

When it comes to sports, we tell our children, "You have to go to practice." If that practice happens to be on a Sunday morning, we may complain that the coaches are not making our Christianity easy for us. But it's because they actually put some value on what they're doing. They're saying, "This is important. We want you here." They're acknowledging that practice makes a difference, and we all have to make choices.

So why can't we make that claim about worship? You can respect the fact that people may choose something else instead. But practice matters in religion, too. When it comes to religion, why is it wrong to say, "No, I don't think it's the same when you don't put any effort into it"? It's okay to say that. In fact, we ought to do it without apology. There's no other area of our lives where we pretend something important takes no work. Why do we do that in the area of religion?

Can you imagine someone saying, "You'd be a great doctor. If you want to do it, you just do it. You don't need anyone else to tell you how to practice medicine. It's already in your heart. I believe in you. Believe in yourself. Just have the confidence. Show the so-called medical world we're not brainwashed into thinking they have all the answers. They can keep their operating rooms and scalpels. You can do surgery. You've always been able to. In fact, I'd like for you to do my surgery, right here on the beach, during this sunset." We wouldn't talk like that—or believe it—about almost anything in life, but think about how often people talk like that about religion.

In other areas of life, we insist that our children go to sports practice or dance class. In fact, we often skip church in order to get our kids to sports practice or games. And then we go to church the next Sunday and complain that the school or the village had practice last week. "Somebody ought to talk to the coaches and get them to fix that." But why is it the coach's job to make your Christianity easier? And why should the coach work around Sunday morning services instead of Muslim Friday services?

And by the way, those coaches who are not making our Christianity easy for us ... that's partly because they're actually putting some value on what they're doing, and they're saying "We want you here." They're acknowledging that this time and energy spent makes a difference, and that we all have to make choices.

Religion is not more demanding than most other practices; in many ways, it's less so. People shouldn't attend church, read the Bible, and pray out of fear or guilt; they should do those things because they take their journey of faith seriously and want to do it with depth. How different is that than going to the gym regularly, playing tennis every day, or becoming vegan?

In cases where people make other choices, we don't need to get worked up and shaming. People make choices all the time. But be honest and acknowledge that you are making a choice. You are not forced to choose football practice over church, or the other way around. You freely choose that. You can say that in football practice there are consequences. You could get kicked off the team for choosing church over practice. Sure, that may be true. But everything has consequences. You could miss a life-changing lesson on a Sunday. You could miss the opportunity to meet someone who is hurting and needs your help.

Chances are your child is not going to become a professional football player. Chances are he is not even going to play for more than a few years. But hopefully your child will be a person of faith for a lifetime, and practice matters there, too. It will take work and some getting used to. Help people understand why you think it matters.

How about saying, "Here's why I go to church," and take it from there, based on our own little treasures? Every community has been entrusted with some treasure that is theirs to save for the rest of God's family. Tell us about yours.

An Anglican might say, "Here's what the *Book of Common Prayer* means to me. It's a little awkward to recite all those words at first, and some of that language, it's old, and it comes from England, for goodness' sake. I'll admit there were times when I felt like those words just crumbled in my mouth like when the seventh grade teacher suddenly called on me to read aloud from Shakespeare and I wanted to die. But there are other times over the years that those words became like poetry and they held me up and they are beautiful. Let me describe that to you."

A member of an intellectually feisty church might say something different. "Let me describe to you the beauty of scholarship and Bible teaching. Let me describe to you these different things we bring to the table. We try to study scripture like Jesus would have done as a Jew. We compare, we contrast, we look up the original languages, we embrace and debate the contradictions, and we learn and grow as thinkers and friends."

But the common denominator in what these members of very different communities would be saying is that this stuff takes work. A meaningful life of faith is rigorous. It's not rigorous like running while being chased by killers; it's rigorous like running track, when you run and run and run all these long runs to prepare for the marathon you may never get to, but the running makes you love running more, even when it's hard and uphill. There's no one explanation for why you love it, really. Maybe it's the endorphins triggered by all that expended energy that are bursting from your brain cells; maybe it's that sense of Zen serenity so often described by runners. The answer is a mystery, but it pretty much doesn't matter, because when you love something (or someone—or Someone), that's the reward in itself.

Rigorous mystery

So what about mystery? Is it legitimate to pursue faith rigorously and still land on "it's a mystery" as a conclusion now and then? It seems to me that if God wanted humans to understand everything, we'd be God.

But we're not God.

God did not leave us with a cosmic library full of concrete answers. We didn't even get left with the same collection, for crying out loud. We all got different books, transmitted orally, written down late and rife with human error. Of course it's mysterious.

Why didn't God leave us the answers, and a practical collection of titles? God could have left us a big yellow paperback called *Divine Knowledge for Dummies*.

Some will argue that those who accept mystery are

just self-justifying and self-involved. I think they are real-istic and evolved. But that's because I accept mystery, so I have a vested interest in seeing that as a very good quality. Which points to the fact that I might be self-justifying and self-involved, too. Oh no.

Religion at its best at least makes you think about this stuff. And mystery is humbling. It implies we don't know. That message rubs like sandpaper against our self-involved, narcissistic culture. We don't have all the answers. And no, we can't make this stuff up.

Atheists will say, "Yes, I can make this stuff up, and you made it up, too; all of religion and spirituality is made up."

Okay, then, let's leave it at that. You can think it's all made up. I can think it's a mystery. And we can both be mad at the people who are certain about things. Because if there's one thing I am certain of, it is that certainty is wrong.

All those points of view can be contained in the world's religions: certainty, doubt, belief, unbelief, ego, and argu-ment. There's always been a healthy flow within the generations, the reformers, the purists, and the pursuers of mystery. I don't have to cover all that territory myself or even in my lifetime because religious traditions cre-ated over time are bigger than anything you could do by yourself.

We pick and choose within those traditions. I love the maddening marvel that all my questions have been asked before. People have thought about these things. We are not the first generation of geniuses.

We could make it up for ourselves but that's not as interesting or rigorous. It's easy to play by the rules of a religion in which you write your own script. It's actually much harder to find meaning in the words of a book we did not write for ourselves, from a very different time. It's easy to create God in your own image and then follow her. Much harder to work with the God who created you, the same God who did not tell you everything you'd like to know and did not even ask for your instructions.

So why bother?

A religion of my own making wouldn't be rigorous. It might be fun, though. I could replace communion with pasta in front of the TV. During Lent, I could preach at length to myself about how wrong everyone else is, and tell other people what they should give up. I could make my weekly offering in the shoe department at Nordstrom, because where you heart is, there shall your treasure be also.

But the church calls me out of idolatry, as fun as idolatry might be. It calls me out of worshipping my every opinion and thought, and into the company of others. Left to my own devices, I would be left to all my own vices.

These days it is countercultural to suggest that anyone might benefit from the company of others in the life of faith, particularly others who have gone before us, in ancient traditions. It's much easier to point out the blind spots of our ancestors in the faith, their missteps around women, sexuality, and things. But we can still learn from the cloud of witnesses who went before us. We can say they lived in a different world, and that they were wrong about many things, but perhaps still right about the God thing.

So when we hear complaints about Christianity, and the media, critics, atheists, and SBNRs paint it with a broad and bigoted brush, why don't we object? Why don't we tell them a different story? Of a progressive church where your questions are welcomed but where we learn from a tradition older than we are. Where we worship a God who invented us and not the other way around. Where we gather in church not to entrap God but to take God seriously in the company of other people.

Generally these critics are working off an old definition of one narrow sliver of Christianity, and they expect me to apologize to them for it. Sorry, but no thanks. I am tired of apologizing for a church I am not a member of. Their bigoted description of church as a box full of backward Christians has worn thin for me. These days, I take these people on with rigor.

Rigorous searching

People tell me they see the appeal of the communities I describe. Even people who have been wounded by religious communities will tell me that they are still open to a life of faith in community that is reasonable, rigorous, and real. But they think I am selling something that doesn't exist in their part of the world. "I'd come to your church," they say, "but there are no churches like that near me."

One of the most rigorous parts of a journey of faith is finding a religious community in the first place. It is hard to find that community that resonates; where a person can sense that they could feel at home, but not too much at home. A good religious community is like that: both comforting and discomfiting. God loves us exactly as we are, and God loves us too much to let us stay that way. That's how religious community should feel, but it won't because that perfect balance is God's alone. We human beings just take a shot at it.

And the way we do that is in worshipping God together with other people, sharing comfort and discomfort, compassion and prophecy, judgment and forgiveness. But first we have to find a place to call home but not entirely at home. Finding that community, like worship, will take work.

Ironically, the pursuit of rigorous religion is in itself rigorous, which is a really hard sell. I can't believe it's worked on anyone, let alone someone as prone to laziness as I am, and I'm not the first.

But finding that place takes work and isn't easy. And when people tell me about their seeking, I can hear the pain and frustration in that journey, the perceived hurts and the all too real ones.

Maybe, after being hurt in one community, they visited one or two other communities and then stopped. So I ask them when and where their search for a church has taken them lately. Usually what I discover is that they haven't visited a church in a long time. It has not been a particularly rigorous search.

Their last experience of worship may be years behind them, even decades, but they feel confident in their knowledge of the religious landscape around them. "There are no churches like that around here," they explain, like amateur sociologists of religion.

I often learn that if they have visited churches, they went once or twice. They don't remember what church it was. They recall the errors made by the clergy, an offensive statement in a sermon, a clumsy welcome, either too warm or too cold. They may recall a sense of being lost and not getting much out of it. They tell themselves they tried, and couldn't find what they were looking for.

But their answers to my questions are revealing to me and often revealing to them. When they actually remember and admit how long it has been, or how few places they actually looked, they are surprised when they hear themselves talking. "Wow. It seems like yesterday," they admit, "but I guess it has been twenty years. Maybe I should go out there again."

If someone looked for a residential home the way many people look for a spiritual home, it would sound like this: "Yes, I know that when I move to a new city, I need to

look for a place to live. Life is better with a roof over
head. But I went to see a couple of open apartments and
I just didn't get much out of the experience. I didn't feel
like the landlords really valued me as a person. Would you
believe they asked me for money? One place was empty. I
couldn't picture myself in it. Another was full of someone
else's furniture, and their taste was terrible. Sure, an apart-
ment is essential but I've looked, and there just aren't any
good ones out there."

Most would agree a roof over your head is essential,
worth searching and working for. You might have to settle,
but you wouldn't give up. You wouldn't give up on finding
a home.

Finding a spiritual home deserves attention, too. It even
deserves a rigorous search. To those who think it doesn't,
don't tell me that you tried once or twice and couldn't find
one. I wish people would just be up front and admit it was
a low priority for them and they didn't put much effort into
it. Trust me, I'm fine with someone telling me that. But
when we care about something, we keep searching.

What if you heard a parent describe a college search for
a child like this: "We couldn't find one we liked, so after
that we gave up. After all, we visited five colleges. After
that, we stopped looking. That was ten years ago with our
eldest. Based on those five visits ten years ago, we decided
not to show any of our other children any colleges either
because, as you know, there aren't any good ones. But later,
if they grow up and have kids of their own, they can make

their own choice about whether to expose their kids to college."

I suspect that college freshmen test even God's unconditional love. But if someone told me they visited a couple of colleges, couldn't find one, and therefore decided college was a bad idea for everyone, I'd probably find myself defending college. And if I actually cared about the person I was talking to, I would tell them that the search for a college, however imperfect, deserved more effort than they had put in by checking out just a few.

But when people say, "I couldn't find a church," we in the church shrug politely as if they have already done their best search. We might even go on to apologize for their fruitless search. "I'm sorry those three churches you experienced seventeen years ago didn't meet your needs. And before you even raise it, let me apologize for the Crusades, the Inquisition, suicide cults, and any other stereotype that kept you from looking further... You clearly tried your best."

It's a response dripping in condescension, first, toward the seeker who is permitted to put forth little effort and engage in stereotyping, and second, toward the community of faith we belong to, apologized for or left unmentioned. In essence we are saying: "I may have a church, but not one I value enough to share with you, who I do not value enough to engage."

Sometimes it just comes down to prioritizing what's worth rigor and what isn't.

Chapter 12

Religion as Real as You Are

I AM NOT A BIG fan of massive revival meetings where people get born again and saved. Mostly because it hasn't happened to me. I hear from others that it's actually a pretty cool experience, but I can't speak to that. I don't have fun at a large stadium watching basketball or rock bands, so why would religion work any better? But for people who have been through it, baptized at a revival, a megachurch, a tent rally, or even these weird spectacles when bodybuilders for Christ break boards and then baptize you, I've heard that it's an experience of a lifetime.

But I also have heard that, afterward, many of the newly saved often wonder what it was all about. Was it the emotion of the moment? The length of the service? The heat? The power lifters for the Lord? Was it really life-changing?

I've met lots of people who have been saved and they

pretty much keep their original personalities, for better or worse. I don't believe that one single moment does it for most of us, even if there is a great musical sound track like this song that goes with it.

Just as I Am

Just as I am, without one plea,
but that thy blood was shed for me,
and that thou bid me come to thee,
O Lamb of God, I come, I come.
Just as I am, and waiting not
To rid my soul of one dark blot,
To thee whose blood can cleanse each spot,

O LAMB OF GOD, I COME, I COME.
CHARLOTTE ELLIOTT, 1789–1871

Old hymns are like sausage: better to consume them and move on without undue reflection. I love "Just as I Am." But like many old hymns I love, I can't think about it too much. And again, like sausage, I prefer to ignore the blood part of that hymn and stick with the yummy first bite, "Just as I am." I really connect with that part.

Many people associate this hymn with altar calls and revivals when, at the end of big emotional rallies, the preacher calls people to come forward and "get saved." In a packed stadium, rivers of people leave their seats and flow down front to receive Jesus as Lord and Savior, and this is the hymn they would always sing.

Billy Graham, the most famous revival preacher of modern times, always wanted this hymn sung during his crusades' altar calls because he believed that this hymn brought him to faith.

So given my skepticism of the events that are so synonymous with this song, I am surprised to love this old revival hymn as much as I do. Whenever I sing it, my heart gets full at the idea that God loves me "just as I am," which I take to mean God loves everyone that way: the saved, the unsaved, the selfish, the selfless, the many religious people, and the Nones. We really are all loved, and we don't have to join any group to get that.

I'm in religious community for other reasons, including getting to hear and in some cases accidentally memorize old hymns that I am not sure I believe, but they seem to believe in me. Especially when I get to verse three, which seems to contradict the first two verses.

Just as I am, though tossed about
with many a conflict, many a doubt,
fightings and fears within, without,
O Lamb of God, I come, I come.

"Just as I Am" was written by someone during a period of doubt. Charlotte Elliott wrote the hymn in England in 1836, and it was included in a book called *The Invalid's Hymnbook*.

Charlotte Elliott was part of a large, vital family who had a great passion for ministry. But she was beset by a series of health crises that left her, at the young age of thirty, a complete invalid. Essentially she could only spend her time in bed or lying on a sofa. Her brother, a clergyman, committed his life to establishing St. Mary's Hall, a school designed to give the daughters of poor clergymen a good education for a nominal fee. The family regularly sponsored bazaars, fairs, and fund-raising events for the benefit of the school. On the eve of a particularly big fund-raising bazaar, Charlotte experienced something like a dark night of the soul. She went to bed, and she felt worthless. She thought, "I'm an invalid. Everybody in this family, everybody in my community, is working for something good, and I can't do anything." She decided that life was not worth living, and she began to doubt that there was a God or a purpose for her life. She was up all night in total despair.

The next day was the big bazaar, and her family and friends would be buzzing with activity. And she lay on a sofa in the drawing room, at a distance, watching all the good work happen. That was when the text of this hymn came to her, and she just started to write, as if she were taking dictation. All of a sudden, out of this place of profound doubt and despair, she wrote a hymn about a God who loved her, just as she was, without one plea.

Today a book with a title like *The Invalid's Hymnbook* could never be published. It would be considered offensive in a world in which no one wants to be considered sick.

But that so-called invalid's hymnbook ended up bringing healing for everybody, because who among us isn't in need of healing? And who among us isn't in need of real community—warts, doubts, and all?

Really searching

I'm a big proponent of serious efforts to find a religious community. So when the host of a Canadian radio show asked me off air how he might find a church like the ones I was discussing on air, I was surprised. He had access to bright and engaging religious figures through his work. He of all people should be able to find a church. "Have you visited any churches lately?" I asked.

"Yes, quite recently," he said, "and I couldn't find one."

"Well, how many did you visit?" I asked, predicting a small number.

"Twenty-one," he said.

"Twenty-one?" I gasped. "Well, how recently?" Was this a professional grudge holder against religion who joined and left churches for every adult year of his life?

"Over the last two years," he said.

"You mean to tell me you have spent the last two years trying out all twenty-one churches in your town?"

"Well, I live in a very small town, and there are twenty-one churches."

"It doesn't sound like you live in a very small town,"

I said, because at some point I wanted to be right about something. "Because small towns don't have twenty-one churches. One thing I am sure of is that you do not, in fact, live in a small town."

"I guess not," he said, giving me that one point. It was the only sloppy thinking I could catch him on. I actually felt pretty awful about my assumptions, especially after he described a thoughtful journey, with observations of what he had learned along the way. He pointed out what was beautiful about one style of worship, and where somewhere else he heard a particularly well-crafted sermon. He had looked into denominations and visited websites. This guy clearly wanted to find a church. He was willing to put that effort into it. He went to visit all twenty-one churches in his town. But why couldn't he find one? Were his standards too lofty? Or was something else going on?

Finally, I asked him, "What was so wrong with them? They don't sound too bad to me. No church has it all. Couldn't you even find *one* that you liked?"

"Oh, it wasn't that," he said. "I liked a lot about all of them. It's just that they wouldn't like me. I've done bad things in my life. I don't belong with those people."

"Didn't they say God loves you despite all that?" I asked.

"Sure," he said. "They all say that. But I don't think I believe it. I can't love everybody. And if they knew me, or what I think, they wouldn't want me there."

He gave me a lot to think about. Somewhere along the way, he learned that churches are places anyone can visit,

but only incognito. If they knew who you really w...,
they'd kick you out. He was looking for a church that was
real. He was looking for a church where he could be real.
Real churches are out there. They're all over the place. But
I could also see why he hadn't found one yet. Sometimes
in religious communities, we save the real stuff for the
insiders—or even worse—we just don't deal with it. Either
way, the outsiders leave feeling as if they'd never fit in.

"It would break the poor pastor's heart"

An ethics professor asked a city minister to assemble a
group of thoughtful businesspeople for interviews on the
subject of business ethics. So the pastor gathered a small
group at church and the professor asked them how their
religious faith impacted their lives in the office and the
business decisions they made. The pastor encouraged the
group to share those difficult gray area stories but people
stuck to the obvious. They talked superficially about not
stealing office supplies or the importance of being a good
mentor. It was only after the pastor left the room that the
real stories started flowing.

These executives had nightmarish tales of deals gone
bad, deception, plant closings, firings without cause, prejudice, and greed. They talked about agonizing decisions
that would never be 100 percent right and how hard it was
to live with the realization that people were being hurt

by choices they made. No matter how they tried to live their values, life was a lot messier than they had been prepared for.

Finally the professor stopped taking notes and asked them, "Why didn't you say all this when Pastor John was in the room with us?"

There was an awkward silence until one of them said, "Oh, he's such a wonderful man. It would just break his heart."

They weren't worried about Pastor John's wrath or even his push back. They saw him as a sweet, naive man whose view of the world was simplistic, almost childlike. They weren't worried about Pastor John being disappointed in them. They were worried that Pastor John would be disappointed by life, and that he was far too tender to take it.

Now, I can tell you that clergy are not easily shocked.

But clergy, like most people, are afraid to tell the truth about themselves in church. So instead they pretend to tell the truth, with trifling little stories that pretend to be revelatory ("Now when I say I like chocolate, I mean I really like chocolate. . . .") but are not really ("Sometimes I think I am a chocoholic!"). Unless the pastor is obese, in which case he won't be talking about food but football instead, or some other such harmless pleasure that really isn't his issue.

Heaven forbid an obese pastor talk about food addiction. Someone at church might actually think they could talk to such a pastor.

Every time a clergy person pulls a punch, an angel in heaven yawns, and the laypeople wonder, "Are these really the only problems our pastor has?"

I can picture the angels up there sighing, "She has all these people there on a Sunday listening to God's word that we are saved and loved no matter what, and then she acts like it barely applies to her. No wonder they don't think it applies to them."

Over time, clergy learn to tell a story in which they are the heroes, or they are the ones who step away from sin, or they sin but in a manner so inconsequential it makes the congregation think they live on Sesame Street. It makes the church seem less real.

Particularly when the Bible passages can seem so harsh. "Get behind me, Satan!" Jesus yells to his best friend and disciple, Peter.

And then the preacher begins to preach with some inane anecdote that wouldn't wake Satan up from a nap.

"My mother always made the most delicious cookies, and we couldn't help but steal one or two before they had cooled...I know, we were wicked...Tee hee hee."

And the congregation titters along.

But somewhere out there in church someone is hurting. Someone is grappling with a bigger decision than whether or not to steal a cookie, or even whether to eat one. Someone has put everything else aside to get there that morning.

They deserve more than a charming anecdote meant to draw them closer to the warm fuzzy preacher with warm fuzzy faults. (What are the odds? We both are *obsessed* with *American Idol*?)

As for the person obsessed with porn, he's out of luck that week, and the next. Never mind that clergy use porn as much as the next guy. I know this because clergy write about it anonymously, in clergy magazines, almost always after the fact. There is one evangelical leadership journal that seems to have a two-year cycle of clergy sins, written by anonymous sinners, after the fact. If it's spring of an even numbered year, it's clergy gambling addiction season. The winter will bring Internet porn. Other years bring marriage problems due to overwork, plagiarism, or clergy mental illness.

Always anonymous, the clergy have been delivered from such sin by the time they write their pieces, but still there is no name attached. The byline says it all. You cannot be known.

So instead, clergy make jokes in sermons about their weakness for donuts or their fave football team and hope that someone can read between the lines and see that they are human, too.

Instead they think, "I could never tell my pastor that. It would break his heart."

Clergy, please tell the truth about yourself. Be real and love me just as I am. Let me change and let me change you. Don't dumb down the message. Respect my God-given brain. Don't lower your expectations of me. Tell me what people have done before, over time and in community, to get to know God so I can try it, too. Don't tell me it doesn't matter but don't scare me into it either. Show me. Love me. Welcome me.

With the eyes of the heart enlightened

When I think of my deepest yearnings for real encounters with faith, real encounters with goodness and evil, real encounters with scripture, of being prompted by the Holy Spirit, I didn't feel them that way at the time.

It's not like I was sitting around celebrating my own life when suddenly I noticed that I was missing the rigorous study of a ten-thousand-year-old book that appears to accept slavery, animal sacrifice, and wife abuse. No, I never thought to myself, if only I had more of that in my life. But when I look back, I can see that I did want a tradition larger than myself, and I've been blessed by a weird book read by weird people through the ages.

No, most of my yearnings show up in retrospect, after they have been met and filled in the most surprising ways. I am shocked to discover the phrase "the eyes of the heart enlightened" (Ephesians 1:18) in the middle of a letter by the apostle Paul, whom I had thought of as a violent sexist thug. Even after his conversion, I objected to many of his ideas, like the notion that celibacy is considered a higher calling than marriage, which is to him basically a dumping ground for lust. I hated Paul's sexual ethic and had avoided reading his letters, but then when I first saw the words "the eyes of the heart enlightened," I thought, they are too beautiful not to have come from God.

When you look for a community of faith, you look with "the eyes of the heart enlightened." That beautiful phrase implies that there are different ways of looking, and in this beautiful way you look with the eyes of the heart, eyes that are enlightened. I presume those eyes are wide open to reality but accepting of the real life they see in front of them, and able to see the beauty in broken things.

Religious community is a broken thing because people are broken things. Both can be beautiful, or they can just look broken. It depends which eyes you use to see.

Showing up is key, and then showing up as our real selves and allowing other people to be their real selves.

Chapter 13

Lost, Broken, and Loved

IN HER FIRST INTERNATIONAL TRIP ever, my twenty-five-year-old mother moved from a small town in South Carolina to Tokyo, when I was just six months old. There we met my father, a foreign correspondent who had taken one day to pick out a house for us in a traditional Japanese neighborhood. A stylish Southerner with a taste for adventure, bouffant hairdos, and high-heeled shoes, my mother soon learned how to speak the language, to bathe standing up, and to collect Asian pottery. As our family went on to move from one country to another, my parents grew their collection of pottery. Since the pieces were arranged around the house just out of reach of running children and frisky dogs, it was not until I was a teenager that I noticed a vase that did not fit with the rest of the collection.

With a cream glaze and a blue Japanese design, it

looked like it had once been a fine antique but now it was badly damaged and glued together. It stood amid the finer pieces, a mass of cracks crudely glued together with what was obviously the wrong type of adhesive—everywhere the twenty or so pieces met one another, glue had bubbled out yellow as it dried, creating the effect of scabrous scars, or a dried-up runny nose.

"Why don't you get rid of that one?" I asked my mother. "It looks just awful next to the others."

"Never," she replied. "It's the most valuable piece of pottery we have in this house."

Then she told me the story.

When I was a toddler, my journalist father covered the Vietnam War, moving in and out of the war zone for weeks at a time. Whenever he returned home, he brought a piece of Asian pottery to add to my mother's collection. The vase was one of the finest he'd found, and he wrapped it in brown paper and string and carried it carefully on several airplanes and buses before finally walking up the driveway with it in his hands.

That was the moment I, at two years old, saw him and rushed forward. Surprised and elated, my father opened his arms. As I fell into them, the vase fell out and smashed into pieces. My father apologized, but my mother had no worry for the gift, she was just delighted to see her daughter and husband together. Later that night, my mother pulled out the glue, clumsily repaired the vase, and pronounced it "precious."

It remains a symbol to me of why so many people loved her, and mourned her passing. There was no situation she didn't think could be repaired and redeemed, including her own illness. It surprised only her by taking her from this world at the age of sixty. She could always see the beauty in broken things, including in me. When I went through a brief stage at Yale Divinity School, attempting to adopt what I thought was the look of a serious student, in baggy dresses and stern glasses, she had to intervene. "Darling, it is wonderful that you want to be a minister," she said, "but I'll be damned if I will tolerate you dressing like a missionary." Most people who had known me as a teenager were shocked, perhaps appalled, to hear that I intended to go into the ministry. My mother claims that she had seen it coming.

She was involved in doing makeovers long before there was a word for it. People were always showing up at our house with three suits on hangers, and asking my mother which one to wear to the job interview. She saw the beautiful possibilities in everyone. So much so that whenever she'd tell me news about friends, I came to know that she automatically and unconsciously gave everyone a promotion. She would describe the resident as a surgeon, the teacher's assistant as an assistant principal, and everyone as fascinating. When her cultured spiritual-but-not-religious friends were disdainful of my strange turn in career path, she defended my choice to lead a dying church where the choir outnumbered the tiny congregation by telling her friends, "It's really very much like being a college president."

But when the reality of life hit hard, and failure crossed, my mother was somehow able to sweep away all those promotions and listen to people who doubted themselves with absolute attention. As a person who had failed herself in more than one arena—from some of her workplaces to her marriage—she was the person you felt you could tell your failure story to and have it blessed. You could trust that she would see the beauty in broken things.

The beauty of broken things

As a pastor, I see my own calling very similarly. Until God gets around to the major repair work, I try to repair the brokenness of the world in small ways. But I wasn't always a pastor. I learned about the beauty of broken things from my mother, who lived out her faith by seeing the beauty in broken people, even me.

I've always hoped that the churches I love can offer a different understanding of brokenness but that doesn't always happen. We are just people, after all. I am as broken as the next person. I take comfort in the sacrament of communion that seems all about the beauty and redemption of broken things. When we gather around the communion table, the vessels, whether pewter plates or delicate chalices, are not the issue. It is in the breaking of the bread, tearing it out of the perfection of a formed loaf, and leaving the edges jagged, that we remember what Jesus said. "This is my body, broken for you." Those words render absurd our human preoccupation with perfection. True beauty comes, not from the flawless piece, nor from the piece that pretends to have no crack.

On the Sunday mornings when I preside at the communion table, I tell the congregation that our salvation lies in God's broken body. But in real life, as I lead a complex organization, I am not so different from any other leader. I fall prey to the same pressures, and the same ambitions. I want my church to be perfect. So in the frenetic pace of children's classes, choir rehearsals, efforts to create more programs and attract more people, a congregation and its minister can forget the beauty of being broken, and appear to be a congregation without flaw or fault.

My mother's great gift of seeing the beauty in broken things pushes me to push my church and all churches to resist the culture of the golden bowl. But so do my own mistakes and brokenness. When we can acknowledge the beauty of the broken vase, remarkable things can happen. The hungry are fed, the homeless sheltered in the midst of affluence, and personal testimony moves from victory dance to truth telling. If we can remember that the broken body of Christ was good enough to save us, we can pull our own broken vases out into the spotlight. We do not accept them as inferior pieces in the collection, but rejoice in the beauty that their imperfections bring to the collective mix.

I once spent a year on the outside looking in. Once a pastor, I became a pew sitter, a mysterious weeper. I was the weird stranger who showed up once or twice but never went to church coffee hour. I was the one surfing the websites for church times, leaving late, getting lost and then feeling embarrassed about bursting in during the opening prayer. There were so many times when I almost couldn't walk in, thinking that if they knew me, they'd never want me, and if they did, would I want them? I had my own resentments. Just like the church visitors I had talked to over the years, I brought them to every church visit with me, like a checklist. I was going to call them broken before they saw the brokenness in me.

But something remarkable happens in traditions bigger than you are. The core teaching had stayed inside me and got called out again. I wasn't preaching about the beauty of broken things. I was hearing it preached. And when they broke the bread at the communion table, I ate my broken bit just like everyone else, and called it precious.

I recall a Sunday afternoon many years ago, back in the suburbs of Chicago, after my mother had died. After preaching, I was at home, wanting to rest. But my aging father was making conversation I was too tired for. He sat at my long clean kitchen counter, littering it with an explosion of newspapers, magazines, coffee cups—all teetering on the edge of chaos. When he gestured to call my attention to an article he was reading, the coffee cup went flying, spilling onto the papers in a sticky mess and breaking when it hit the floor.

"I'll get it," he said, using a magazine as a mop.

"No, Dad, it's okay," I said, in a tone that indicated it might be time for him to leave. "I'll clean it up after you're gone."

After he'd left, I picked up the pieces of the broken coffee cup, mopped up the papers, and pulled out the spray-on cleaner. As the fumes of disinfectant hit my nose and the counter shone once again, I breathed a sigh of relief.

That was the last time he drank coffee at our counter. I could not have known that I should have paid more attention that night, worried less about the mess, and perhaps had him stay awhile longer. My counter sparkles. But I want the mess back. I want to see the sticky rim of a coffee cup, mop up newspapers read and discussed and stamped with a date of a happier day.

Often real isn't pretty, but it is beautiful.

Now that my father is gone, I preside at another unfinished meal, once again in the clergy role, behind the communion table. And there my brokenness finds its place in the open arms of Jesus, and my eyes are opened in the breaking of the bread. Clean counters, golden bowls, and perfect people are no match for the broken vase that now sits on a grown orphan's mantel. I still have the broken vase my late father dropped when he saw his young wife and me, his child. Glued together by my late mother, it is now up to me, their only child, to tell its story. The broken vase's beauty lies in the scars themselves, reminders that over the generations, God has picked us up, put us back together, placed us back on the best shelf, and called us precious.

Still lost

I often feel like I'm lost, not in the existential sense, but in the very mundane sense. I have a very poor sense of direction. Some would say I have absolutely no sense of direction. I envy people who instinctively know where north is, and they can just feel their way driving around a neighborhood, trusting their instincts.

I have learned I cannot trust my instincts. In fact, when I get lost, if I have a strong inclination to turn left, I have learned that instead I may as well turn right, because statistically speaking, that is more likely to be correct. Whatever way I think I should go, I should go ahead and pick the opposite way to save time, and then I ask for directions. I look for a shepherd to get me back to my flock.

One blustery winter, the weather back home in Chicago caused all the incoming flights to be canceled, and I was about to be stuck for at least twenty-four hours in Des Moines. As flights continued to get canceled, it became clear there would be only one source of deliverance, and it would not be an airplane but a bus. I decided to catch the next bus to Chicago: the Megabus.

You'd think a Megabus would be easy to find, but it wasn't. I'd been told the bus stop was located in some industrial parking garage just a five-minute walk from my hotel, and the bus left at twelve thirty. Knowing that I'm not great with directions, I left at eleven forty-five to give myself forty-five minutes to do a five-minute walk.

So I went out on my walk, and you know what happened. Before I knew it, I'd gotten distracted and I'd forgotten some of the directions, and I realized I couldn't figure out where I was. So I had to ask for a shepherd to help me. I was lost. I stopped people on the street, and I said, "Where is the Megabus stop?" but nobody knew where it was. That should have been my first indication.

They finally found someone and they directed me. It was quite a long walk away, so I was walking very quickly. It was many blocks. I walked about ten minutes, got there, and there was no Megabus stop. I only had thirty minutes to get there now. They said, "Oh no, it's back the other direction." I found myself walking back in the same direction I had come from, and there was no stop there. Then I asked more people, and they sent me off in a different direction.

Finally, about thirty-five minutes had gone by, and I had about ten minutes before the bus was leaving, and this man said, "I promise you if you stand at this bus stop, the Megabus will come. I've seen it here a million times."

I said, "I can't believe it's true. On the Internet it said it was in a parking garage. This can't be right. This can't be right." I was standing there thinking that somewhere else from here the bus was going to come and go, I was going to miss it, but he said, "Do not leave this spot."

No bus appeared. For five whole minutes.

And then this strange little tiny trash vehicle moving very slowly caught my eye. It was about the size of a golf cart and these two big guys were crunched into it. The back was piled high with trash cans, all stacked on top of each other like the Leaning Tower of Pisa. I waved the strange vehicle down and it coasted to a stop in front of me. "Look, you guys have to know the city backward and forward. Is this the Megabus stop?"

"Well, it used to be the Megabus stop a few months ago, but they moved it," the driver said. "It's all the way across town now."

"How long would it take me to get there?" I asked.

"You can walk in half an hour."

"The bus is leaving in five minutes. I'm stranded here. I can't get home. You gotta help me." And I poured out my heart, about how much I wanted to get home, how I always get lost, how I left extra time that day, how nobody seemed to know where the Megabus stopped and the unfairness of it all. The next thing you know, one of the guys is getting out of this little vehicle and making room for me to sit up on the gearshift. They had to take some trash cans down and leave them on the curb to make room for me and my suitcase, which they wedged in between the remaining cans. "We're going to get you to that bus," the driver of the golf cart announced, with the confidence of the captain of the Starship *Enterprise.*

So they put it at full speed, which on a golf cart, is like seven miles an hour. We're going through red lights and going around huge trucks. We were not fast but we were nimble. They got me to the Megabus three minutes before it left.

I didn't have time to get their names or to thank them formally. They were tossing my suitcase to the curb like an empty trash can and yelling for me to run for that bus.

We are not in charge of our own itineraries. Any sense that we are is an illusion. We are all just a bunch of lost sheep trying to get home, but it's so much better if we are real with each other and help each other along the way.

The Lord is my shepherd

The image of God as a shepherd runs throughout scripture. "The Lord is my shepherd; I shall not want."

It's the classic good news–bad news joke. The good news is the Lord is my shepherd. The bad news is I'm a sheep.

So much so that, later, pastors were called shepherds and the congregations their "flocks." But what exactly does a shepherd do? It's a job description the ancient Israelites would have been familiar with, and so would the early Christians have been, and so would be much of the world throughout its history, for our society has for the most part been much more agrarian.

But in this weird moment of time, in this strange place, in this current world of agribusiness where only a few farmers spend time on the land or in the company of animals, we've become increasingly distant from this image of the shepherd. These days, very few animals are given the chance to wander in green pastures. Many lead short miserable lives in factory farms. This image of God as a shepherd perhaps calls us back to a better way of being stewards of the earth and of the creatures on it.

If you ever *have* gotten to see a flock of sheep in a field, it's a beautiful sight, even if it's just a photograph. In my mind, I picture the scene like this: The shepherd is an Irishman with gray-flecked hair, Wellington boots, a worn tweed jacket, and a wool cap. There are a few cheerful sheepdogs running around his heels until that moment when he gives a subtle signal and the dogs run ahead, knowing magically what to do.

The sheep viewed from a distance are these beautiful white fluffy dots on a country landscape. They are little clouds in a sky of verdant green grass, and there on the horizon the quaint local pub rises like an oasis. That's the fantasy, but if you ever get up close, sheep are a very different matter.

They are not white, but they are usually very dirty and

soiled. Their coats are not a bit soft and fluffy so much as tangled and matted. You would not want to snuggle with them. They smell terrible. They make weird and frightening noises. Lambs are cute; sheep, not so much. But if the shepherd is God, you know who we are.

We're those sheep, lovely from a distance but messy, smelly, and a bit dim-witted up close. Yet God gets up close. The central message of the gospel is that God decided to come to earth in human form to be a shepherd. Jesus uses the imagery over and over again. He speaks of human beings as being these lost sheep, and God has a special place in his heart for the sheep that wander and will even seek after them. And then comes the image of Jesus as a lamb sacrificed on the cross.

That image is so powerful. It's that image that prompts one of my favorite songs from the Taize community in France: "Shepherd me, O God, beyond my wants, beyond my fears, from death into life."

Perhaps you've seen in the Roman Catholic Church the pope or a bishop carrying a symbol, this large stick with a hook on the end. It is a shepherd's crook. It's meant to be that rod or that staff that the shepherd would use to pull the sheep back into line. "Thy rod and thy staff they comfort me," the Twenty-third Psalm says.

So the shepherd's crook is not a weapon, but it's a tool to keep the sheep safe as they make their way to green pastures, because it's comforting to think that someone is guiding you. It's comforting to think that somebody else knows the way. It's comforting to know that you are not lost.

Later in church history, the pastor became the shepherd. The origin of the word "pastor" (think of the word "pastoral") is Latin for "shepherd." When I was a pastor, I had a stole that was given to me, cross-stitched by a member of a church in Connecticut early in my ministry, and sewn into it was the symbolism of the lamb now glorified with a crown in heaven and over it a shepherd's crook. Pastors love the word "pastor," or "shepherd," but the clergy had no business claiming that word. The Bible passage is pretty darn clear. God is the shepherd and the rest of us human beings are 100 percent sheep. That includes the clergy.

There are no stories about sheep rescuing people, or speaking a secret underwater sonar language, or coming when called by name, or finding their way home across the country accompanied by talking kittens. Sure, sheep get prizes, but not for any real accomplishment other than weight, wool, or mating. Sure, they can win beauty contests, but I have yet to hear of a sheep that distinguishes itself intellectually. No one says, "Sure, most sheep are dim-witted, but this one sheep can speak sign language." No, there is no advanced placement track for a sheep.

So as long as we're all one another's furry flock-mates, at least we can aspire to become shepherd seekers. We try to shepherd one another. We bring one another back from being lost, all in the name of the God who shepherds us, because nobody likes to be lost. But let's be clear: That's our hierarchy, not God's. God thinks of us all as sheep and loves us anyway.

Real work

I love Saint Paul's idea that we're all different parts of one body, each of us with a role, so that no one person has to do it all. I came to read his stuff differently once I realized they actually were letters. He didn't know he was writing something that would get read out loud and out of context two thousand years later. He thought he was writing to people he knew, about their lives right then and there.

Paul's letters were actually written to small groups of people, who were probably meeting in someone's house, in someone's living room, talking about Jesus long before we had a word for that, like "Christianity." These letters would encourage them to follow Jesus, learn about him, pass on the stories from his short life. But they were just letters from one guy to some other people he couldn't talk to personally so he wrote to them instead.

In some cases, he sounds like he really misses these people. In other cases, he sounds utterly sick of their petty and feuding ways, and he tells them that in no uncertain terms.

Once you realize these are real letters written to real people, it makes sense that the most common subject is community and how we get along with one another. You're all parts of the same body, he explains, but one of you is a foot and one of you is a nose so you are going to come at things from very different angles. Get it together, people. Stop telling the foot to develop a sense of smell. It's not going to happen. Work it out. Paul's letters are very real, but also hopeful, aspirational. What if, instead of criticizing the other parts of the body, we praised them, and were grateful for them? What if we all tried to do our own thing well and stopped judging everyone else's performance?

Take this snippet from Romans 12:8–10, where the church in Rome gets an earful.

> If you preach, just preach God's Message, nothing else; if you help, just help, don't take over; if you teach, stick to your teaching; if you give encouraging guidance, be careful that you don't get bossy; if you're put in charge, don't manipulate; if you're called to give aid to people in distress, keep your eyes open and be quick to respond; if you work with the disadvantaged, don't let yourself get irritated with them or depressed by them. Keep a smile on your face.
> Love from the center of who you are; don't fake it. Run for dear life from evil; hold on for dear life to good. Be good friends who love deeply; practice playing second fiddle.

You can take that advice into any aspect of your life, whether it's the church, your workplace, or even your family. It's hard to live with one another, in community, in intimacy, and then on top of all that, it's hard to follow Jesus when he's not around anymore. These letters gave practical advice on how to live together and do that. They are real letters to real people, and we read them in church two thousand years later because we're real, too.

Chapter 14

Silos and Sound Bites

INCREASINGLY, AMERICAN SOCIETY IS HIGHLY seg-
mented. For example, we're very segregated by age.
When you're at an age where you have young children,
you're socializing with people who are parents of kids at
your kids' school, and then all of a sudden you're in this
other place and you don't have friends in that age bracket.
There are just so many forces pulling us toward segrega-
tion. Even how we get our media.

We don't all have to read the newspaper anymore. We
don't all have to watch the evening news, because I can get
my news from this television station that represents points
of view I already hold. I can watch Fox News. I can listen
to NPR. I can go to this website. I can even get a direct feed
that only sends me the commentators I already agree with.
Does anybody see that this is a product of a culture of nar-

cissism? Nobody has to compromise, and we are increasingly siloed, spending our time and energy with others just like us. No arguing, no compromise, no challenges, no change, no growth.

Heaven forbid you go to a religious community where someone does something irritating, and you're offended, because it has been a long time since you've had to deal with anybody you disagreed with...up close. There are those terrible people on television, but you can turn them off. So religious community rubs like sandpaper against the culture of narcissism, and no wonder people howl and complain.

The other thing religious community does that is a real no-no in a culture of narcissism is it hearkens back to a tradition bigger than we are. Today, we live with the freedom to choose our religious path but there is a shadow side to that. It is the self-centered message that whatever I feel or experience is paramount. Some of that comes from deconstruction where people were appropriately criticizing ideas of objective truth and logic in the academy, and saying, "Guess what? That wasn't objective. That actually only represented a small elite group, and they're mostly male and mostly white."

But then, you go from this healthy deconstruction to an unhealthy obsession with personal experience that leaves us saying "And therefore nobody can say anything about anything, so whatever I feel is true."

"So why did you do that?"

"Well, I felt like it."

"Why did you *not* do that?"

"Well, I didn't feel like it, and I have to respect my own truth."

But guess what? We're capable of being selfish and mean and losing our tempers. What mediates that if all we do is celebrate our every instinct? Religious traditions seek to temper that and suggest that folks have been thinking about these things for thousands of years.

In a rigorous and reasonable and real community of faith, those standards should not feel oppressive, but more like the hopes you have for someone you love. God can love us and therefore want to spend time with us, where we're actually paying attention, not just to God but to all the generations God spent time with before meeting us.

Locked out

Chicago winters are horrible, this one particularly so. It's an icy night in the parking lot. It's dark, and I'm trying to get in my car. I'm carrying all these books, and I'm in a bad mood. It has been a long day. My locked car won't open. I'm clicking and clicking and clicking. It won't open. I'm clicking and clicking, and getting madder and madder at that car door. Finally I'm about to kick the thing. But instead, I put the books down, on the wet ice, and when I put my hands on that frozen door handle, I realize it's not my car. I was clicking outside the wrong door. Here I was, frustrated and angry, cursing a door that wouldn't open because it wasn't mine in the first place.

I actually believe that many Nones and SBNRs have the experience of clicking outside the wrong car. They're doing something. They have an instinct to try to open themselves to a channel of power that will unlock something and get them where they need to be. They're not opposed to what we're talking about; they're not shut down. But they've had the experience of clicking their key to unlock a door without success. We might say, "You know what? Maybe this is not your car over here. Your car might be on the other side of the parking lot. Let's go and try it there."

What I learned at the Gay Christian Network

The Gay Christian Network is a very interesting organization, founded by an evangelical Christian who was raised Southern Baptist. As a teen, he went to his pastor and told him that he thought he was gay. The next thing you know, his parents had signed him up to be "helped" by an ex-gay ministry, which did him enormous damage and harm. He ended up going to a Christian college, where he came out and came to terms with his sexuality and with the fact that God loves him as he is—as a gay man.

When I was invited to speak at the Gay Christian Network convention, I knew I'd probably gain more insights than I'd share.

In the churches where I've served, we have worked to welcome and affirm everybody, regardless of sexual orientation or gender identity. Those congregations went through processes that took time but they ended up becoming "open and affirming," which meant they went on record welcoming everyone long before states were legalizing gay marriage. That's the hard and important work of the church and I'm grateful to have had a chance to do it. But Justin Lee's church world is very different, and so was the group of people at the GCN convention, where they were coming from church environments in which being "open and affirming" was out of the question.

I had been invited to bring my book, *When "Spiritual but Not Religious Is Not Enough,"* to these attendees, most of whom came from very conservative Christian backgrounds, many of whom had been profoundly wounded by the church. I was supposed to be talking about why religious community matters. I didn't know how this would go over.

The worship service was very much in the vein of that (stereotypical) worship style with the big screen and words to songs that were not familiar to me but would be familiar to people who are familiar with that tradition, which once was called "contemporary worship" but is now way too old to be called that.

It seemed to me that many of the songs were about blood,

jarringly accompanied by rather cheery videos and Power-Point pictures of rainbows, waterfalls, and sunsets; and everyone sang along in what appeared to be full agreement with the lyrics. I was never raised in a conservative Christian environment. I don't get a warm fuzzy feeling singing about "Him" in that "Jesus is my boyfriend" music genre.

I wasn't trying to look bored but perhaps I did, because a woman turned to me and said, "I know this isn't your tradition, Lillian, but this is powerful. It's meaningful because this may be the only chance some of these people have to worship in a setting like this—where they can be who they are, hold their sweetheart's hand, and experience this and these special songs. They don't necessarily want to go to another church that's entirely foreign."

It was like she had read my evil and limited mind. That's exactly what I had been wondering. Why didn't they just dump all this oppressive stuff and come to my church instead? We'll do your gay wedding and spare you these blood songs with rainbow slides. It was a win-win. What did they have to lose?

Her words reminded me that we all have a lot to lose when we are attached to a worship style, a theology, or a belief system. And we may not want to lose it. It was arrogant and simpleminded of me to assume they all wanted just to jump on board my little ship.

That changed my speech the next day, and afterward, there was a Q & A workshop, and the room was packed. We had one of the best discussions I've ever had on this topic. These were people with theological rigor and passion. They want to shape the church, they want to find a church, but many of them don't have a church. For them, coming to the convention of the Gay Christian Network was as close as they could get to the experience of coming to the church where they'd grown up and were most comfortable.

The devil's dichotomy

Many of their questions and comments were in this vein. "I was raised in this very conservative Christian tradition, and I keep trying to find a church where the worship style is like that because I truly felt the power and presence of God there. I meet with the pastor, and the pastor says, 'Look, you can come to worship, but you can never be in a position of leadership, cannot be a member in full standing, and we're going to encourage you to join this ex-gay ministry.'"

Another person said, "I hear that there are churches that would affirm me, but I've heard that I probably wouldn't want to go there because you don't experience the power of God there." In some cases, they referred to the mainline Protestant churches that I was a part of as "the bland leading the blind." I object mightily to the idea that the only Christians who experience passion in their faith are the ones who wave their hands while singing lyrics projected on a PowerPoint. But that was their comfort zone and they wanted it in their worship.

Their dilemma was such a sad one, so antithetical to the concept of Christian love. They could either attend church where they could experience the power of God, but not acceptance of who they are. Or they could attend church where they were affirmed but really don't experience the power of God.

One after another, they asked, "Which church should I go to?" I had to really think about that one. But then I realized it was a bad and simplistic question, a devil's dichotomy, because there's no right answer to that. I answered, "I don't think you should go to either one. I think you need to keep looking. I don't buy into that false binary. I don't believe that you can't have both. You may have to put some more work into looking, i.e., it's going to be rigorous."

When I quizzed them about whether they had sampled the variety of the religious marketplace lately, they admitted they hadn't been to all that many churches. They may have been to a Lutheran church when they grew up, but haven't been back in twenty years, presuming it's as dull and dry now as it was then.

The Holy Spirit is doing a wonderful thing in American Christianity right now, and we've just loosened up. In the old days, the New England Congregationalists of *Mayflower* heritage would never have paid attention to liturgical seasons. They'd never have had an Ash Wednesday service. And there was a deep theological reason for that—because that's what the Catholics and Anglicans did—and the Congregationalists hated them.

So many of the decisions that churches have made in history have not been positively based, but negatively based. "We can't do that because these other people do it."

Or "Here's why we're great, we don't do what those other people do..." Instead of talking about what we actually do and why.

There's a wonderful thing happening right now—there's a new freedom. Part of it is because of all the different backgrounds of people who now participate in church—people who were raised as Roman Catholic, Evangelical, Mormon, or raised with no religion, can all end up in the same place together.

I used to think that all evangelical churches are conservative, but that's changing, too. I don't think I'll ever like singing songs about blood while looking at rainbows on a screen, but who knows? All bets are off these days. You can't characterize churches by their brand or the sign on the front door. Everything is becoming more fluid.

I began to form an answer to the devil's dichotomy question posed to me at the Gay Christian Network, and it began sounding like this: "Look, when you're stuck with that dilemma, I'm not going to tell you to go to one church or the other; I want you to keep looking. I think there's a third church out there where you're going to experience the power of God; but I do not want you to go to a church where you're going to be treated like a second-class citizen, because that is denying the power of Christ that is working within you. You have to keep looking.

"There's another possibility to consider," I added.

"Maybe you were meant to go to this church that doesn't quite fit you right now. And because you're in it, it will change. Because of your history and your gifts and your passion, and your musical taste, people's lives are going to be changed. It's not just about meeting your needs. Maybe there's a church that needs *you*."

They laughed, they argued, and they took me seriously. They also talked about amazing experiences of God in very imperfect religious communities. They didn't buy into the devil's dichotomy any more than I did. If and when they find their new churches, and their third way, I want to go to those churches, too, waterfall slides, blood songs, and all. They gave me so much hope for the church that I wanted to close my eyes, wave my arms, think about rainbows, and sing about Jesus.

You have a choice

I don't believe that all the SBNRs and Nones have decided that Christianity's hypocrisy and phoniness make it ineligible as a valid avenue of faith. Some of them may say that, but they say it in the way the people at the Gay Christian Network said it, with all the passion and feeling that comes from being in a relationship with something you miss. To point out the obvious, they were spending a week at a conference with the word "Christian" in it, and it wasn't the Society for the Abolition of the Christian Faith.

But they had been told in various settings of the church that they could not be real about who they were. If they were out as gay or transgender, they couldn't be in church leadership or work with the kids. They had to lie in order to be eligible for those roles!

Naturally, they saw the hypocrisy. I am sure they also saw leaders with feet of clay, behaving abominably as people are capable of doing.

Good questions

They had some good questions, like: Why does that married serial cheater get to be in leadership but not me?

When the Baptists come to town for their annual conference, why are the hotel bars empty but the liquor stores full of pastors brown-bagging it back to their lonely hotel rooms?

These are reasonable questions and they are real.

At their worst, these questions are just tools for blame and shame. If you ask the question to expose hypocrisy but then answer your own question with an immediate "Gotcha!" you might want to look at that.

Look, the Baptist pastors drink. Look, people cheat on their spouses. Turn on the lights, expose the little rats, and chase them out. Gotcha.

That's an ugly way to use those questions. Expose humanity, yes, but remember, it's our common humanity.

At their best, questions like these are windows into one another's humanity.

You cheat, too? You hide your pleasures, too? You get disgusted with the rules? You don't live up to your best hopes for yourself either? You are afraid of being judged by people like me?

If we can ask those questions in a real way, church community can be a place where we pray for what we really need. One person can pray for a more faithful marriage while another can pray for a world that has room for couples who do it differently, who don't always march two by two.

We can stop monitoring who gets to sit on what toilet in which bathroom and let people be and pee as they want. There are bigger plumbing issues for the church to worry over than North Carolina's bathrooms, like how Flint, Michigan's, water got poisoned and why people of faith should care.

Searching without stereotypes

Many of us approach faith as a journey, which is appropriate. In my congregation we say, "Wherever you are on life's journey, you are welcome here." We don't think of faith as a destination, a place where you arrive once and for all. It's a journey with a beginning, but as for the end? That's for eternity. Faith is a journey.

For some people, the faith journey is tourism, a place you stop by temporarily. You know what it's like to be a tourist. You fly in knowing that pretty soon you can fly out. You observe the new country, you take pictures, but you don't get deeply involved in the people's lives there. Tourism is a journey with clear boundaries and limitations. And for some people, this is how they approach faith. Like tourists, interested in sampling the fare along the journey, but not ready to dig in.

But there's another way to take a journey that is very different from tourism. And that is the journey that is an adventure. When you travel thinking of yourself as an adventurer, the journey is going to be different.

When you are a tourist, you approach the trip with a certain set of expectations. I want to see the Taj Mahal and get my picture taken in front of it. I want to drink a fruity drink on the beach. I want to attend a beautiful worship service and be moved by it.

When you're on an adventure, you have to relinquish your expectations. Expectations are the enemy of adventure. If faith is an adventure journey, you need to accept that you may not know how this trip is going to turn out. You visit a country that might be strange to you, and off the beaten path. You cannot control the itinerary. You may be less concerned with having canned, prepackaged experiences, and more interested in being stretched to learn new things. You may, on an adventure, actually join a church and try to meet other people, some of whom will disagree with you, or even annoy you. That's an adventure.

The early followers of Jesus might have started out as tourists, pretty sure of what they'd see and hear, learn and do, with him as their guide. But they discovered that faith in him was a nonstop adventure. There was no playbook for church, no set of doctrine that everyone had to believe. No itinerary. Jesus was a man to them, and when he died, they had the biggest shock of their lives. Death did not swallow him up, but he was raised from the dead. Talk about a whole new travel itinerary. Before that, they thought they knew where the journey of life ended—and that would be death. But in the resurrection, they realized that death might be the beginning of the very biggest adventure of their lives.

Are you clicking outside the wrong car?

Before you give up on religious community, consider that you may have been clicking outside the wrong car. That church wasn't a bad car, but it wasn't your car. Maybe for a time it was your car, but now you need a new car. For all of those people clicking outside the wrong car or religious community, frustrated, as a church, as Christians, we have a story to tell, and it's a story of a practice that is rigorous, reasonable, and real.

Now when I say that, I do not believe we should come on strong with a message about hell and damnation. First, I don't believe it. I absolutely do not believe that heaven is restricted to members of any one sect or religion. Oh

God, I hope it's not. How tedious that would be. And the people who have thus far avoided church are not going to be attracted to that idea anyway. So let's just admit that intellectually, emotionally, and theologically, the "burn in hell" argument has had its day and we're glad it's over.

But what does a believer say to someone who is leery? The opposite of judgment is *not* saying nothing, or worse still, saying something vague.

I'd rather listen to a harsh person than a vague one

Sometimes when asked about Christianity, and in reaction to the "burn in hell" people, we end up annoyingly vague, saying things that we hope imply that we don't judge anyone for not attending church. So we say, "Whatever floats your boat. To each his own," or we say nothing at all about our own commitments and longings. We hide in generalities, thinking that we are complimenting the person by being so nonjudgmental. But that response is just another way of saying, "I don't care enough to engage you."

But when someone tells a story about a locked car door on a cold night, you should say more than, "Oh well, just skip driving then. To each his own."

Because they've just shared something real. And if you know what it's like to have found your car in the lot, why not share that?

Just as a car owner doesn't need to know why one electronic key works and another doesn't—he just needs to have the key that works for him—we don't need to have a degree in theology to know what works for us, and what our car is. So if you like your car, why wouldn't you share that with someone who might not have found one that they like?

Take the risk of telling your own story of the cold night in the parking lot, your dark night of the soul, of admitting you've been there, of wondering, "Maybe you've been clicking outside the wrong car." And if they come with you to church, don't assume the worst. Consider the fact that they might be thinking that all this is amazing. They are hungry to worship something bigger than themselves. They feel that hunger in others, too. They get fed by the word and feel the pulse of the spirit. They come back because the intervening days are richer and lighter when they bracket their lives with an ancient book and prayers. They see that religion is not something they do once a week, but what God does all week long.

Worship is their chance to connect outside of time and space with God and then see every moment differently. They begin reading the Bible only to discover that one day it flipped and the Bible started reading them. Sacred stories became the lens through which they see the world, like prodigal sons, prophets swallowed by whales, orphans without a home, all grounded in God, centered in worship, and free to dream.

By being in worship and going deeply into a life of faith, we are better prepared to experience the divine everywhere else in the world. It's not about building up this institution. That's not the point of it. It has to be about preparing people to experience the divine and to do the divine will and to create good and beauty and truth and to live life abundantly when they're outside the building, away from the institution. To do that, we have to have a generous spirit about the really weird ways God works.

Here's how it has worked for me: I want to be grounded in God, centered in worship, called to serve and free to dream. I think other people may want that, too.

Back in my apologizing days, if the conversation continued in that vein, people often came around to liking the version of church I was describing. But looking back, I can see it was a conversation of critical distance in which both parties kept God at arm's length. I was apologizing for a sport while selling them on a team. I was burying the lead.

In journalism, they teach writers never to bury the lead. The lead is the key point of the story—begin with it, or you will lose the reader. You only get the one chance to capture the reader's interest in line 1, so if the story is about a forest fire that took place yesterday, don't begin with, "Throughout the ages, there are as many ways to create firewood as there are yearnings in the soul of humanity for warmth..." That's burying the lead.

I think about that a lot as I look at how we talk or don't talk about our faith. Back in my days of apologizing, I might never have told anyone about experiencing God, in church, in worship. There was no time to talk about worship, let alone experience it. I was too busy debating, apologizing, and engaging on the head level, trying to convince people that we were open-minded *about* God rather than simply open *to* God. I came to it honestly. My listeners encouraged me.

I used to joke that we were the church most likely to be attended by the people who don't go to church. People thought that was funny, especially the people who didn't go to church. They laughed, too.

But I don't think it's so funny anymore. I think it's sad. I buried the lead.

Chapter 15

Grounded in God, Centered in Worship, Free to Dream

S O WHAT DOES IT MEAN to have the power of God within you? There's so much in American culture that is superficial around the topic of "power" and "personal power." There are so many people in the religious world peddling versions of Christianity that bear no real relationship to its mystical practice. I cringe at the televangelists and their "prosperity gospel," the guys on TV who promise that if you just sit there passively watching their show and send in a little money and listen to their CDs, "You'll experience this personal power and prosperity."

There's nothing about that in scripture. It just doesn't work that way—it's so much more complicated. Eventually you will hit Good Friday, when our savior dies on the cross at the age of thirty-three. This is not a self-help religion.

Power source

But everyone wants self-help. There are plenty in the New Age world who imply that we have the power to control our own lives simply through our thoughts. If we can control our thoughts, we can control the universe around us. Good luck with that. It's just another side of the same coin—an expression of superficial "religiosity," a product of our culture of narcissism. "It's all about me. I am the power source."

There are times in our lives when we really do feel powerful. Think about some time in your life when it felt like every door was opening, the world was your oyster, that every door you knocked on was open, there were possibilities everywhere, things were just working, and you felt powerful.

Then, there are times in your life when every door you knock on is closed, and you don't feel powerful, times we don't feel strong and when we don't feel well physically. There are flu epidemics that outsmart the vaccines, diseases like malaria whose simple causes we don't seem to be able to prevent, and illnesses whose origins are elusive with cures nowhere in sight, painful losses of mind and body to Alzheimer's and heart disease that have nothing to do with our attitude, but with our mortality. To date, no one has the power to prevent death.

Sometimes we get confused about what we have power over and what we don't. When we feel as though we don't have power over something, it can be very frightening, we feel very alone. We could find comfort in each other, in God, if we could let go of the myth that we could be in charge.

Because most of our fears are not original or unique to this moment in history. The desire to be in control is as old as the world. And one way we confront that is to test ourselves against the rest of the world, by exploring, traveling, and experiencing whatever we fear, while at the same time clinging to other people who are along for the same wild ride.

Power loss

Which is how I found myself in a tree house in a remote jungle in Nicaragua, scared and surrounded by screeching animals. Pulling up to the dark lodge after midnight, the host declared, "I'm sure you're exhausted and far too tired for an orientation. So I'm just going to show you to your tree house and leave you there." Suddenly I was not exhausted. I was ready for that orientation of the facilities. But instead we were hiking up this mountain in the total darkness. It's taking forever and ever, I'm hearing howler monkeys and other animals I hadn't even thought of being afraid of in advance.

And I wasn't even there to do anything good or meaningful. I was in this jungle on vacation, and it was a cheap one, at that, hence my strange arrival in the dark after midnight, sans orientation.

Finally, after hiking this long, invisible path in the night, we come to this bridge we have to cross in order to get to where the alleged tree house is. This is a suspension bridge, about three feet wide. It has wooden slats that you can see through, and you hold on to this rope, and it swings as you walk across. Since it's after midnight, I'm grateful in a way, because I can't see what's below. Our guide locks me in for the night, and says that he will give me the orientation in the morning.

I turn on the lights and start reading all these brochures that tell me about all the poisonous scorpions and snakes I might encounter. "Don't worry," our guide had said as he left. "Those critters are more afraid of you than you are of them." I can tell you without a doubt that this was untrue.

I did not sleep well that night. I just lay there listening to all the screeching and scratching of all the so-called frightened animals. I had never before considered monkeys to be vicious but I now considered this idea for the first time: The most intelligent species have the most brain capacity to plot against us humans and these monkeys had probably been doing just that.

Why didn't those poisonous scorpions and snakes take out those noisy monkeys? Because they were afraid, not of me, but of their monkey overlords who were plotting humanity's destruction, beginning unmercifully with those of us who chose ecotourism for a vacation. Ah, the irony. That incredibly deep thought kept me awake until it didn't.

The next day, I woke up to this incredibly beautiful vision. I was in that amazing tree house surrounded by flora and fauna, looking out over this incredible view of the ocean. The monkeys were quiet, the snakes and scorpions were probably at an assassin's meeting, and all I could see was beauty.

Walking down the path from the tree house in daylight, I finally got to see the suspension bridge we had crossed the night before. I was glad I hadn't seen it back then when the monkeys were taunting me; that would have pushed me right over the edge. Because in daylight I saw the swinging, swaying rope bridge was strung up hundreds of feet high over an enormous gorge.

The next night I was more peaceful in the tree house, reading by myself and watching the sunset. This was heaven as I imagined it. The sun finally set and I turned the lights on to keep reading. It was so calm and beautiful. But then, all of a sudden, all the lights went off. Alone in the tree house, I was in utter darkness, in a jungle, where the monkeys were yet again yammering plots against me, now that the sun was down, and they had switched the lights off. My heart stopped and then started again as I sat up straight with a jolt.

And the lights came back on. I breathed deep and sat back again with my book and continued to read. Then, all of a sudden, the lights all went out again. I sat up straight, and they came back on. Then it hit me: I'm staying in a groovy ecolodge and there's a motion detector on the lights.

I know what to do: When the lights go off, I'll just move, I think. The monkeys aren't in charge. I am. All the same, I don't want to be alone in this tree house in the dark. I think I'm going to make my way down the path, across the suspension bridge, and join civilization—the other people in the lobby area. There are plenty of lights along the path as well as along the suspension bridge.

I take a deep breath and head across the suspension bridge. But when I get to the midpoint, all the lights go off. I'm in the middle of this bridge, in the dark just swaying in the wind. I'm holding on to the ropes because I'm terrified, but I know what I have to do to get the lights to come back on: I have to move.

I have to convince myself to let go of the sides. So finally, I let go of the ropes and wave my hand, and nothing happens. It's still dark. So I think, maybe I'm not making enough motion. Soon I'm waving both hands, hanging over in the dark, trying to move the entire bridge enough to make the sensors turn the lights back on.

But nothing is happening. I'm hanging in the middle of this suspension bridge in utter darkness, and I don't know how long this is going to go on. The motion detector is broken, and I'm just stuck here. I'm powerless. Totally without the power to control it, until I finally realize that I do have a little power. I don't have to stay there in the dark. I can move forward, as terrifying as it is. I just have to put one foot in front of the other and get across this bridge, and go find some other people.

So I do it, and it's the longest walk of my life. It probably takes me ten minutes to go those last thirty feet as I'm shaking in the dark on this bridge that is swaying back and forth. Of course, when I get to the other side, and put my foot on firm ground, all the lights come back on. I am relieved but that feeling is soon replaced by outrage. What kind of operation are they running here? In the jungle, in Nicaragua, in a tree house ecolodge...

No, no. I couldn't think rationally about it; I was trying to stay mad.

I finally got to the lobby and grabbed the first I person who worked there I could find. "You guys have to do something about these lights. I just had a pretty scary experience out there, waving my arms like crazy on the suspension bridge, trying to get the power to go back on but nothing happened. You have to fix those motion detector lights."

The employees and other guests looked confused. Finally, the manager said, "We don't have any motion detector lights here. That was a power outage, Lillian. We have them all the time. Um...this is Nicaragua."

Then people who had been there awhile began to laugh. "Did you think you were controlling all the lights by waving your arms on that bridge?" Suddenly, I pictured myself out there in the dark on that bridge and I was laughing, too. Poor old God sees us doing all that goofy stuff all the time. I hope God gets to laughs, too.

What a moron I must have looked like: waving my arms while trying to cross the suspension bridge, as if to say to the universe, "I will now turn all the power of Nicaragua back on. Okay, I'm moving my arms, open sesame!" What a goofball.

This strikes me as a metaphor for our narcissistic modern life. We have all these choices, all these things we think we can control. We can even get ourselves to a tree house in Nicaragua and choose the two- or the three-meal plan.

We think we have all the power—that we're the power source—and all around us, other frightened people are telling each other, yes, we have all the power. We're the power source. Well, I was not the power source. The power source was three hours away at a Nicaraguan power plant with spotty service and I was on this bridge out in the jungle. I wasn't the power source. I had it all backward.

I also was not entirely without any power. None of us are. In my tradition we talk about the power of Christ working within you. God is the power source, and we can't control the power source; but the power of Christ working within us is how we respond to what happens around us.

I did not have the power to turn the power source back on and off to control those lights, but I did have the power to ultimately decide to put one foot in front of the other and respond to the situation by walking in the dark.

And now, like so many human beings before me, I carry this little story in my heart, next to other stories, all of them clumsy encounters with the Holy Spirit. It expresses a truth bigger than we are; two mysteries at once:

We are not the power source. And we have God's power within us.

Why would I want to apologize for that?

Real people, real work

The same church that inspires us to do better should have room for us at our worst. Whatever your addiction, idolatry, sickness, or sadness, you are welcome here.

And if we really have to pray out loud for everyone's body parts, let's give them all equal airtime, penises, gallbladders, and brain chemistry. Because if we're listing illnesses, I want depression out there getting the same airtime with cancer.

Or we could drop the laundry list and trust that God hears everyone's prayers, whether we inform God or not. We could just ask for healing of mind, body, and spirit.

From a church pew, we can see things about the people we're sitting with, like the fact that they didn't brush their hair in the back that morning or that their children's shirts are inside out. I remember once a parishioner told an usher that one of our worshippers that morning, who he recognized as homeless, had shown up drunk. The usher's response was perfect. "It's not like the rest of us don't show up drunk here on occasion. We just get a shower first so it's not as obvious."

Religious community that is real takes work and some hard conversation.

We need to be honest with the people who are not sitting in church but may be looking in from the outside. Admit to them that it's going to take work, much of it caused by the failures of the other human beings in the room, including you. It may take more than one try.

We will disappoint you. I am sure of it. But I'm not going to apologize for that in advance, any more than I can apologize for any group foolhardy enough to open its doors to other people: That's called *community*. It's the root of the word "religion."

Dig in

Worship isn't an escape from the world. It's a way of being in the world. It deserves more explanation than "whatever floats your boat."

It also doesn't deserve to be forced on people. Worship should be freely chosen and lovingly offered. So if people have a perception that religious life is shaming, judgmental and fear based, let's tell them something different. You can make an intelligent argument about why religious community matters without saying that the other person is going to burn in hell.

Life is not a garden party, and everyone will experience pain. But is that all there is? Or have people been wrestling with this stuff for a long time? You don't have to be out there on your own. You have a choice. Look around. There are so many beautiful options in the religious landscape that are reasonable, rigorous, and real. People who put down roots in one tradition bigger than themselves are explorers too. It's okay to dig in.

There is an alternative to make-it-up-yourself spirituality. It is called a mature faith, practiced in community over time, grounded in God, centered in worship, called to serve and free to dream.

Real love

I hate the violin. I should know. I played it for eleven years and quit with alacrity.

But I do know a good violinist when I hear one, and one day as I rushed toward some incredibly important appointment with myself, I passed a little girl playing a violin on the street.

She was better than I had ever been, and she played with confidence. But she was no Itzhak Perlman. She had her violin case out for tips just like a grown-up busker, but there were not many coins there and no bills in it at all. I felt sorry for her.

But I had no time to correct that problem. Someone else would have to support the arts. I was trying to get to church. I wasn't leading church, I was planning to attend. Which meant I was running late and had to get myself to this service right now.

Right after I went to Walgreens. It's fun not being in charge.

Well, apparently it was a very short service, or maybe security in Madison, Wisconsin, was at def con code red, or maybe I can wander around a Walgreens for longer than the average vespers service lasts...but by the time I got there, every door to the church was shut and I was locked out.

So I walked more slowly this time, the way I had come, and there again, I saw the same little violinist up the sidewalk, sawing away in front of her empty case.

I was a block away from her when a man stepped out in front of me on my path, standing between me and the girl, his back to her and his face lowered to speak in a loud whisper right to me, "You see that girl playing the violin, up there?" I must have gasped, startled. "I didn't mean to scare you. But you see that kid up there playing the violin?" I nodded. "Could you please give her this?" he asked, thrusting a crumpled-up dollar bill into my hand. As I uncurled it, he nervously looked the violinist's way to see if she was watching, but she was immersed in her unprofitable craft.

"Just toss it into her case," he said. "And whatever happens, don't tell anyone that I gave it to you. Just drop it in and act like you just enjoy the music."

So I did exactly that and it felt great. I may have been locked out of church, but I liked the warm feeling of making an offering as a patron of the arts. I thought that maybe I could come back later with some more money of my own. I could spend the whole evening walking back and forth in front of the child, showering dollar bills on her and proclaiming the good news, "Somebody invisible loves you!"

But that would have blown it. It would be breaking my promise to her dad.

At least I think it was her dad. It had to be her dad, or her teacher, or a family friend. Or a threatening predator. Good God, had I participated in a stranger danger trap of some kind?

No, no, it felt too sweet. A predator would want credit for the dollar, and a predator would deliver it in full view. The man who gave me the dollar bill had to love the kid enough to be anonymous. It was the weird backward affirmation that only a selfless person could want to give to someone very special.

That night, as I watched the little girl playing her violin, I recalled the roughest patches of my own life. I knew what it felt like to have an empty violin case and no fans in sight.

Then, I thought back to better times, when my violin case seemed full of tips that I assumed I had earned through my own talent and hard work. Now, I saw my best efforts as no better than the little girl's.

As she sawed away on a difficult instrument without much expertise or much applause, I thought that this was the mediocre violin playing that only a father could love.

Maybe our biggest fan out there is God, who supplies all the praise that we mistakenly think we earned. God hates to see an empty violin case as much as we do. But rather than fill it for us, God comes at it sideways, occasionally stepping in and convincing total strangers to stop, listen, encourage, and care for one another.

So that one day, when we need it most, we can tell each other without any apology, "Somebody invisible loves you and always has."